Chinese Legal Translation and Language Planning in the New Era

Xiaobo Dong · Yafang Zhang

Chinese Legal Translation and Language Planning in the New Era

Springer

Xiaobo Dong
Nanjing Normal University
Nanjing, Jiangsu, China

Yafang Zhang
Nanjing Normal University
Nanjing, Jiangsu, China

This work was supported by the National Social Science Fund of China Key Program of 2020–"*Research on Chinese Rule-of-law Terminology with Chinese Characteristics Translation and International Rule-of-law Discourse Ability Construction (20AYY008)*".

ISBN 978-981-19-8447-1 ISBN 978-981-19-8448-8 (eBook)
https://doi.org/10.1007/978-981-19-8448-8

This Springer imprint is published by the registered company Springer Nature Singapore Pte Ltd.
The registered company address is: 152 Beach Road, #21-01/04 Gateway East, Singapore 189721, Singapore

Preface

Since the Reform and Opening Up Policy was proposed and solidly implemented in 1978, the legal translation in China has embraced radical changes in the past four decades. From entry into the WTO in the 1980s, China has started to introduce its traditional legal culture and achievements in rule-of-law construction to the outer world. Since the convening of 18th National Congress of the Communist Party of China in 2012, gradual improvement and completion has taken place in building the socialist legal system with Chinese characteristics. As a national strategy, Chinese Culture "Going Global" was put forwarded. Being the indispensable part of China's rule of law culture, traditional Chinese legal classics and modern laws and regulations are all important proponents of China's rule-of-law modernization. It is also the need of times for China's traditional legal classics and laws and regulations to actively going global, contributing China's experience and wisdom concerning rule of law to the world, developing the image of a major responsible power under rule-of-law with Chinese characteristics, and enhancing the soft cultural power of China.

To realize the aforesaid goals, translation of traditional legal classics and modern laws and regulations plays an important role in light of practical experiences. This book tries to present a full picture of development of Chinese legal translation by making a comprehensive and interdisciplinary analysis on the translation history of both the ancient Chinese legal classics and the modern laws and regulations. The legal translation in China has undergone twists and turns in the past and always lacked a systematic and comprehensive theoretical framework. Therefore, guided by the language planning theory, this book intends to build a theoretical framework for study and practices of legal translation in the New Era and offer several feasible translation strategies and methods. By this book, the students can get a comprehensive understanding of how Chinese legal language and legal translation evolves, know well about the experiences and problems to be resolved in the current stage, and have access to the frontier information, ideas, concepts, arguments, and theories in the fields of legal language, legal translation, and language planning.

Nanjing, China

Xiaobo Dong
Yafang Zhang

Contents

About the Authors

Xiaobo Dong is Professor at School of Foreign Languages and Cultures of Nanjing Normal University and Specially Invited Researcher at Institute of China's Modernization of Rule of Law. He is also the Director and Chief Expert of Jiangsu International Rule-of-law Research Center, as well as the Chief expert on major projects of the National Social Science Fund of China. His research interests include history of Sino-west civilization exchanges, legal linguistics, legal translation, language strategy and planning, and cross-cultural communication. In recent years, he has published over 150 interdisciplinary academic papers in prominent journals and more than 70 books, including academic monographs, edited volumes, and translations.

Yafang Zhang is Ph.D. Candidate at School of Foreign Languages and Cultures of Nanjing Normal University and Researcher at Jiangsu International Rule of law Research Center. Her research interests include Sino-west civilization exchanges, legal linguistics, translation of Chinese legal classics, and language planning.

Chapter 1
Semiotics, Language and Law: The Linguistic Turn in Jurisprudence

1.1 Introduction

To understand the nature of the law, people normally are faced with two questions: one is that what the law is and the other is what the law should be. The school of natural law takes the natural law as the basic yardstick for judging the positive law. The school of analytical law highlights the scientific nature of jurisprudence and deems positive analysis as the guiding principle of its academic studies. The school of sociological law regards social analysis as the goal of its studies and pinpoints the investigation of the relationship between law and social reality. The above mentioned three schools of jurisprudence reveal the distinct pathways of law studies from different facets, facilitating people to observe legal issues and explore the meaning of law from different perspectives (Hu, 2005: 20).

Law and language are closely related. The law is expressed by virtue of language, which in turn gives specific meaning to the law. Also, language molds the law into something powerful that influences or dominates people's thoughts and actions (Wang, 2001: 1). Hans-Georg Gadamer, the German philosopher, once said: "Whoever has the language has the world" (Gadamer, 1976). Language does not only make man become the intelligent part of the universe. It is not too much of a stretch to say that language is exactly the universe, meaning that the world exists in language and its meaning. In ancient times, people required both a means of communication and common rules for living together. The former is language while the latter becomes laws, which specifically refers to unwritten law or customary law. The law is one part of the world, but in a sense, it is also a "world" by itself. Therefore, the "world" constructed from language lies in it. In the latter half of the twentieth century, as the study of legal issues went through the progressive phase of ontology and epistemology, it was discovered that neither the ontological commitment nor the epistemological turn could resolve the complex connection between "lex ferend" (established principles) and "lex lata" (actual situations). However, what hinders people's legal understanding might be the problem of language, and the way to link individual and object. Many scholars and thinkers, therefore, turned to language as

X. Dong and Y. Zhang, *Chinese Legal Translation and Language Planning in the New Era*, https://doi.org/10.1007/978-981-19-8448-8_1

the category of objectivity, which had been only regarded as a tool of daily communication. As a result, western law studies stepped into the stage of forensic linguistics, that is, the normally called linguistic turn of jurisprudence. Hence, Arthur Kaufmann, Professor at the University of Munich, and Neil MacComick, the successor to the new analytical school of law, proposed: "The law is simply a matter of linguistics" (Shu, 1995: 348).

The law is a unique semiotic system, which constitutes the important part of the social semiotic system. For human being, in order to develop the legal semiotic system catering to their own needs, they have to seek the semiotic materials for constructing the legal world from the society and hence put their own pursuit on these symbolic carriers. Generally speaking, signs have to be mainly dependent on the material carrier, and the objective physical world and even the body and conduct of humankind can all become the symbolic carrier of the legal world. Needless to say, materials and conducts have provided important semiotic carrier for the law. However, there is also a kind of symbolic resource which is of importance and peculiarity, that is, language or words. Law cannot exist without language. Language itself is a kind of semiotic system artificially created by human being. Language is the indispensable building materials for formulating laws. By virtue of language, the symbolic facet of law becomes apparent. Meanwhile, law is not merely the accumulation of language or words but is the normative content within itself. In other words, laws are formulated by the use of language, and they are not a set of signs but a certain criterion of human conduct. Therefore, it is better to say that laws are the semiotic system with normative nature, which can express the characteristics of the laws more accurately. The formation of legal semiotic system is also the process of symbolization. The symbolization of law naturally bears close relation with human being's capacity of using signs, and it at the same time is constrained by the internal nature of semiotic structure. We have to admit that the symbolic function can contribute positive influence on the law. On the one hand, the diversity of signs can provide the possibility of clear and accurate expressions of the law. On the other hand, the use of the expressive signs by the law can promote the realization of the aim of social integration and development of social order (Niu, 2015: 95). Semiotics, as it is often claimed, is a branch of philosophy. Others claim that semiotics is a branch of rhetoric. Still others claim that it is a branch of linguistics. What is claimed, according to Roberta Kevelson, is that semiotics is not a branch of any other discipline-specific mode of inquiry. It is a distinctive method of investigation in and of itself (Kevelson, 1987: 8).

1.2 The Linguistic Turn of Western Jurisprudence

Overall, western philosophy has witnessed two significant turns. The first is the epistemological turn from the seventeenth century onwards, with Rene Descartes' philosophy as the turning point. In essence, it is the shift from an ontological inquiry into the origin of the world to an epistemological inquiry into "how man gets to know". Since then, reason had gained its supremacy in philosophy. The second is the linguistic turn that took place at the beginning of the twentieth century. The so-called linguistic turn represents that the language itself, originally as a vehicle to convey "consciousness" and "concept", defines and constitutes them. Therefore, language becomes the subject of theoretical investigation, as well as the starting point of theoretical development. This cognitive paradigm and methodology were imbued with the whole humanistic studies, thereby shaping the linguistic turn with a holistic effect. This linguistic turn can be traced back to Ferdinand de Saussure, the founder of structuralist linguistics, who argues that all linguistic signs consist of signifier and signified. The former is interpreted as the physical form of language while the latter refers to the concept and value. As language exists before human beings, its meaning is determined by the differences between linguistic signs rather than by men. As Saussure once said, there is only difference with no positive terms. In other words, there is only difference in language without absolute meanings. The relationship between signifier and signified is totally established by convention in an arbitrary way. Jacques Derrida, a famous deconstructionist, also argues that there is no defined boundary between them, because language itself embodies various meanings. It only represents specific and temporary meaning based on the context. Moreover, it cannot guarantee truth that is definite, eternal, and single, while the so-called truth is nothing but the product of our willingness to be seduced by language (Du & Zhang, 2001: 32).

1. Hart's Semantic Analytic Jurisprudence

The history of western scholarship in the twentieth century is the "imperial era of linguistics". Therefore, linguistics is no stranger to jurisprudence described as "a discipline that can never be self-sufficient" by the famous American justice Holmes. The emerging schools, such as, the semantic analytic jurisprudence represented by Herbert Hart, the new rhetorical jurisprudence by Chaïm Perelman, and the popular legal hermeneutics, largely gained the intellectual support from linguistics. This is why it was called "linguistic turn of jurisprudence" (Chang & Zhu, 2003: 65).

Ludwig Wittgenstein, the Austrian philosopher, is a major figure in this linguistic turn. In his later philosophy, he questions and attacks the research method introduced by Plato, who wishes to find common, consistent, and essential properties of things (i.e. the "desire for universality"). This method aims to examine the meaning of a word in a certain linguistic game and identify its similarity and diversity. This requires the basic two steps. Firstly, we should conduct the analysis by putting language into practical daily use and through using it under the context. Secondly, we should avoid ignoring their differences by virtue of family resemblance or commonalities. Instead, it is recommended to replace normative and definitional methods with descriptive and enumerative ones. In law studies, Wittgenstein's daily language analysis, namely philosophy of language, has changed the previous grand theoretical narrative and blazed a new trail for the linguistic turn of law studies methods (Li, 2005: 85).

The English jurist H. L. A. Hart, one of the core members of the Oxford School, is regarded as an outstanding representative of successfully applying the philosophy of language to analyzing legal issues. In his works such as *Essays in Jurisprudence and Philosophy* and *The Concept of Law*, he pointed out that the meaning of legal words and concepts do not remain unchanged, but vary in multiple forms in accordance with the contexts, conditions and approaches. Only by figuring out the contexts and specific conditions under which they are used can we determine their real meaning. He has preferred to adopt a version of the Wittgensteinian notion of "family resemblance", in exploring the relations between different uses of the expressions of "law" and "legal system". For Hart, therefore, the structure of language is important for the methodology of jurisprudence. While he has paid only passing attention to the nature of signs, it is clear from his account of the workings of legal language—including the "penumbra of doubt" which attaches to the interpretation of general terms—that (even while abandoning the command theory of law) he continues to see the legal system in terms of a communicational (rather than significatory) system (Jackson, 2010: 6).

British Glanville Willams and American Watter Probert further investigated the ambiguity in legal semantics and the emotional character of legal terms. Probert proposes the concept of "word-consciousness" among lawyers and judges and regards language as a major tool for social control. Hence, justice is defined as the choice of different premises guided by words (Dong, 2006: 206). Hart severely criticized the traditional defining method in jurisprudence. He states that one should not answer such questions as "What is right?" and "what is legal entity?" in an abstract way, but interpret them by clarifying the context and conditions in which they are used. Hart also quotes J. L. Austin, the philosopher of semantic analysis, that in search for legal definitions, we "do not just focus on the words, …, but also on the real objects to which the words refer. We are deepening our perception of phenomena through thorough knowledge of words." He points out that jurists should not establish legal theory merely on the basis of definition, and they should try to analyze how law and legal language is used in daily life. He also stresses the method to applying semantic analysis to jurisprudence. Hart's inaugural speech marks the formal entry into semantic analytic philosophy of jurisprudence. It becomes the methodology of post-war judicial positivism and leads to a new movement, that is, semantic analytic jurisprudence (Zhang, 1996: 96).

Since then, inspired by Michel Foucault and others, law was understood by P. Goodrich as a linguistic space and a field of discourse, parallel with economics, ethics and aesthetics and so on. In addition, he tried to understand the internal structure of law, including legal modes of reasoning and the lexical system specific to jurisprudence, in relation to other linguistic fields. In this way, legal pluralism with its diversity and uncertainty is truly defined, thus demystifying legal discourse. As such, Richard Allen Posner asserts that the belief of law kingdom is dead (Zheng, 2000: 52).

2. Perelman's New Rhetorical Jurisprudence

The traditional western rhetoric has always treated language as a tool, which means that people convey their meaning by language. There is a natural correspondence between linguistic signs and the meaning of language, and language, the carrier of meaning, is transparent. Belgian linguist and philosopher Perelman in the twentieth century introduced new rhetorical jurisprudence, which incorporated the theoretical ideas of pragmatism and existentialism, especially the philosophy of linguistic analysis. It transcends the traditional theoretical framework of rhetoric as a whole and grants rhetoric a new meaning and a new theoretical system, thus breathing a new life into traditional rhetoric. Specifically, rhetorical theories from ancient thinkers such as Plato and Aristotle have been interpreted and elaborated in a new way, embracing them with new vitality and functions. The core theory of the new rhetorical philosophy of law lies in its theory of justice. It features the synthesis and reconciliation of specific notions of justice through semantic interpretation in an attempt to reach a universal concept of justice. The new rhetorical jurisprudence deems language as an act subject to the constraints of social context. They argue that fact is not the only determinant of semantics, and the meaning is decided by the collective action such as political organization, court decision, occasion and ceremony. To illustrate the application of his so-called new rhetorical legal thinking to the judicial process, Perelman takes the regulation of "no vehicles into the park" as an example: suppose that the gatekeeper is a judge who allows a person with a pram into the park on the grounds that a pram doesn't apply to the rule; And when there is a person suffering heart attack in the park, he lets an ambulance into the park on the grounds that it is the circumstance beyond human control. In this case, the judge does not implement the article mechanically, nor does he merely interpret the meaning of the vehicle. Actually, he makes a decision by the intellectual tool of rhetoric based on social belief and value (Shen, 1983: 78). Although Perelman's new rhetorical jurisprudence remains controversial in both jurisprudence and linguistics, it still offers a unique perspective to learn judicial practice and rule of law ideal.

3. German Hermeneutic Jurisprudence

Another influential force in the linguistic turn of jurisprudence is from Germany, including F. Schleiermacher (1768–1834), Hei-degger (1889–1976), Hans-Georg Gadamer (1900–2002), who has created philosophical hermeneutics. It has been hailed as an alternative way of interpreting the world besides scientism and methodology. Hermeneutics, as an auxiliary discipline to theology and jurisprudence, belonged to marginal discipline in ancient Greece, just as grammar, rhetoric, logic and poetics. Considering from hermeneutikos, its Greek etymology, it involves three interrelated meanings: expression, interpretation and translation. Medieval hermeneutics interprets the meaning of biblical classics in order to understand God's intentions embedded in the Bible. Its methods include textual criticism, syntactic analysis, and contextualization. Its object refers to the "original meaning" hidden behind the words. With the boom of European Renaissance and the Religious Reformation, hermeneutics is no longer confined to interpreting the Bible, but extends from art, law, history, and literature to all areas that interact with mankind and the world. Nowadays, hermeneutic approach is widely accepted and applied, thus gradually becoming a general methodology of the humanities. Modern hermeneutics is a philosophical and cultural trend popular in the west after the 1960s, with "understanding" at its core, being a theory of probing into the understanding and explanation of meaning. Heidegger, the master of hermeneutics, starting from traditional hermeneutics, has transformed it from the passive medium style of language tool into the being of language ontology. Therefore, it turns hermeneutics from spiritual science into a kind of philosophy. Gadamer discovers the respective functions of the author, text and reader, with emphasis on the historicity of the text. He argues that all texts are historical in nature, as they are created in a particular historical context. When reading them, readers are subject to "preconception" and "prejudice". As a text is always the product of society and history, readers may not understand the author's intention despite a good grasp of its social and historical background. Legal interpretation entails loyalty to the text, which requires the interpreter to explore the socio-historical limits of the text and its author. The normative content of the law must be formulated by the existing circumstances to which it applies. To understand the normative content correctly, the legal practitioners must have a historical understanding of the original meaning. The jurists cannot ignore the original intention of the lawmaker, nor can they be entirely restrained by it. The jurist should also consider the historical significance of the law each time it is applied after it has been made, but equally free from such limit. The jurists merely "supplement" meaning instead of creating it. Their task is to "ensure the uninterrupted continuity of the law and preserve the tradition of legal thought" (Gadamer, 1999: 418–424). Hermeneutic theory is firstly targeted towards the understanding and interpretation of works of art. However, there are many similarities between the analysis and interpretation of works of art and legal texts in the process of application by the judge. Hence, modern hermeneutics serves as a reference for the application of law. Influenced by philosophical hermeneutics, German jurists such as Kaufmann, Hassmer and Larenz actively used its methods in their studies on the philosophy of law. "The jurists introduced philosophical hermeneutics to substantiate their claims consciously or unconsciously. This is typically manifested by the debate on the certainty and uncertainty of law and the objectivity and non-objectivity of legal interpretation" (Xie, 2003).

4. European Structuralist Semiotic Jurisprudence

Another influential school of jurisprudence in the linguistic turn is the European structuralist semiotic jurisprudence, which espouses Saussure's semiotic theory. Semiotics, by definition, is the theory and method of studying signs. European structuralist semiotics is created by Swiss linguist Ferdinand de Saussure. From the perspective of Saussure, Foucault and others, language is no longer a product of human practice, but in itself a mode of practice, exerting a decisive impact on other human practice. Furthermore, some scholars regard language as a semiotic system, an "invisible hand" dominating the pattern of human development and the difference of historical background. Semiotic jurisprudence comes into existence when semiotic methods being applied to the law. In its most abstract sense, the characteristics of European structuralist semiotic jurisprudence can be briefly summarized as follows. Firstly, law is a sign. It not only refers to the concept, principle and theory of law, but also a process of reasoning and realization, as well as a specific provision. Secondly, legal signs have their own structure, including a surface structure and a deep structure. The former means what is presented on the surface of law while the latter means what generates the law and creates the meaning. Sometimes, it is referred to "grammar" or "descriptive grammar". The intermediate structure is what lies between the above two structures. It is sometimes called social level, a form of social knowledge containing narrative types and social evaluations. Thirdly, the process in which the meaning of legal signs occurs is the structures and functions through which the meaning of the law is expressed (Lv, 1999: 260–269). Since its inception, semiotics has been regarded as a methodological approach and a meta-science that can explain any problems. The semiotic analysis of legal theory includes both the semiotic analysis of legal concepts and terminologies, as well as legal theories and doctrines. In other words, signs represent legal phenomena, concepts and doctrines. The legislators' activities are a process of putting signs into function. Therefore, the process in which judges decide cases is full of signs. In short, the law itself is a sign. The legal activities are a process of communicating signs. There is correspondence between Semiotics and Jurisprudence, which mainly includes three aspects. Firstly, there is the correspondence of the interpretive function of the semiotics and jurisprudence, because both are interpretive discipline with interpretive theory and function. Secondly, the semiotics provides a micro perspective for the interpretation of jurisprudence. As an analysis tool, semiotic jurisprudence views the jurisprudence as a whole set of system of interrelated signs, on the basis of which the analysis is conducted on the correlation of the individual signs. Thirdly, the application of point of the correspondence lies in the object of the rights. As the object of the rights is the converging point of individual will and interest, it is also the natural starting point of the application of semiotic method in the jurisprudence (Guo, 2012; Guo & Zou, 2012). Semiotic jurisprudence aims not to establish a complete law theory nor plump the "truth" of law, but focuses on how the meaning of law is formed. To be more specific, it offers a new approach and paradigm for law studies rather than a complete theory.

Though there is a diversity of research methodologies and expression paradigms of linguistic turn of western jurisprudence, the common concepts that are widely used mainly fall into four types. (1) signifier and signified. This is Saussure's binary division and he prefers this way, being similar to such pairs of division as language and parole, meaning and value, synchronic and diachronic, internal and external language etc. Obviously, the pair of signifiers and signified is the most famous one. By using this binary division, one can interpret the relation between language and philosophy and society and law. (2) sign, index and symbol. This is Peirce's preferable trichotomy. By using Peirce's semiotics in a dynamic way, the scholars afterwards would rather use the semiotic elements of sign, object and interpretant to analyze the semiosis. (3) encoding and decoding. If we probe into the meaning generated by the symbol in a dynamic way, the semiotics itself can evolve into a kind of information engineering. Legal activity is also a process of information publicity. Legislators give the written law to the judges, and the judges apply the law to the specific cases. Encoding finished by the legislators is to transform the will into legal norms, while the decoding done by the judges is to apply the norms to the legal reasoning of every case. (4) surface structure and deep structure. The surface structure is the content of text or the image expression, while the deep structure represents the cause-and-effect relationship between crime and punishment.

As for what research methods are adopted in semiotics studies, the theoretical circle has not given a definite answer. As we can see from the expression of research methodology of semiotics, semiotics is not only considered as a theory of interpreting symbolic phenomenon, but also a kind of methodology. Niu Yubing summarizes three kinds of methods for semiotics. (1) the method of symbolic restoration. This is the basic method in semiotics, which can be divided into four steps. Firstly, starting from the basic gene of the social phenomenon, that is, trying to probe into the symbolic elements of the social phenomena. Secondly, considering the symbol as the combination of signifier and signified. Thirdly, restoring the generative meaning of the relationship between the signifier and signified. Fourthly, exploring and interpreting the encoding rules of the social and cultural background. (2) the method of structural and functional analysis. This method in essence is to turn the study of linguistic phenomena into the study of unconscious deep structure. By incorporating the concept of system, this method pays much attention to the relation between different terminologies and aims at finding the general rules. In doing the structural analysis, it is also indispensable to analyze the functional relation among the different elements in the entire system and also the relation between the internal and external environment. (3) the method of hermeneutics. From the perspective of hermeneutics, symbol signifies the process and the process of symbolic exchange signifies the certain symbolic encoding and decoding process. As understanding and interpreting is an everlasting open process, the understanding and accepting of symbols should be put into the much broader social sphere. We not only have to consider the sender and receiver of the signs, but also have to consider such influential factors as objects, texts, media, codes, context etc., so as to investigate the whole meaning and effect of the signs (Niu, 2015).

1.3 Two Traditions of Legal Semiotics

Language is at issue in all regards. Legal semiotics concerns all meanings in legal language. A semantic analysis of all major legal concepts is the ultimate task of legal significs/semiotics (Broekman & Backer, 2013). By legal semiotics, also called semiotics and legal theory, or semiotic jurisprudence, it refers to the theory of the application of the views and methods of semiotics to studying the legal problems. The theory of semiotics and law was originated from the beginning of twentieth century and became mature in 1960s. Up till the 1980s, some specific academic monographs and activities of association gradually emerged among American and European scholars. Normally, legal semiotics falls into two categories. Without being dogmatic in this approach, one could venture the idea that there are two traditions within the legal semiotics movement, which embrace different techniques, goals, philosophical and cultural roots and languages. The first one is the legal theory based on the Greimasian semiotics, which is developed by the linguist Algirdas Julien Greimas from the school of Pairs. The second one is the legal theory based on the Peircean semiotics, which is developed by the American philosopher Charles

Sanders Peirce. The task of the legal theory of semiotics lies in studying how the legal semiotic system is employed to convey the legal information among its users (including the workers and non workers of the law). In other words, its main aim is to study the characteristics of legal semiotic system and legal information, the holistic structure of the law (being referred to legal texts, legal discourse or legal argument etc. in terms of the terminology in semiotics), and the conducts of using the legal signs by the law formulators and implementers.

1. Legal Theory Based on the Greimasian Semiotics

Greimas stands firmly in the tradition of European semiotics, strongly influenced by structuralism. He develops and applies notions taken from Saussure, Jakobson, Hjelmslev and so on. His object is not the interpretation of texts, but the explanation of the underlying structure of signification, that is, how the meaning in them is generated (Jackson, 1985). Or rather, he highlights the semantic analysis of symbolic texts. In legal sphere, semantics normally refers to the source of the meaning of the body of law and its ordinary nature. By the use of the theory of Saussure, Greimas divides the legal discourse into two levels, namely, the syntagmatic level and the paradigmatic level. Through the static and dynamic analysis of the structure and function of legal discourse, he attempts to discover the "legal grammar" hiding behind the legal phenomenon. Here, Greimas stresses more about the conducts of legislators and judges.

As far as Greimas is concerned, legislators and judges are indispensable parts of legal semiotic communication with their own roles and functions. Legislators play the role of message senders expressing the national will with its conduct of saying. On the other hand, they are also the final receivers of the communication process. Legislators appear as the subjects and objects of legislative texts. They behave through the lexicon of discourse so as to establish and maintain a type of legal culture. In legal texts, legislators are not only the providers of the legal capacity (such as corporation law) and the institutor of its will, but also the certifier of this subject capacity and the controller of sustaining this role. As a result, legislators in the legal texts are the developer of pluralistic and complicated roles. By virtue of the conduct of legislation and name of the legislators, the symbolic object without judicial semantics has been turned into the one with judicial semantics. Law by its nature has the re-generation procedure of certification and it continuously participates in practicing to certify this procedure. The conduct of the legislators only generates a potential judicial world, which will be realized when the judges apply it (judicial certification conduct). Till this, the original senders of the legal information (legislators) have been replaced by the supplementary senders (judges). In applying the law, judges not only certify the position of legislation discourse in the legal discourse, but also turn them from the ordinary legislation information to the special judicial information, thereby establishing the relationship with the actual social life (Lv & Xu, 1991).

The main scholars of the legal theory study based on the Greimasian semiotics are from France. Another representative scholar named Bernard S. Jackson from Britain also paid much attention to Greimasian semiotics in his monograph *Semiotics and Legal Theory* (1985), which is the application of European continental semiotics to analyzing the legal problems. The basic structure of this monograph includes three parts: (1) the author elucidates Greimasian semiotics and law; (2) the author probes into the theory of legal theorists including Hart, MacCormick, Kelson and Dworkin respectively by the use of the method of semiotics and points out the weakness in their theories; (3) the author tentatively puts forward the semiotic model of law. In Jackson's opinion, the linguistic philosophy deployed by Hart stands in some important respects at the opposite end of the spectrum of semiotic theories from that of Greimas. Hart is interested in communication, viewed as consciously intentional act, and not in signification. Hart adopts ordinary language assumptions regarding the relationship between words and external referents. He regards the contexts of language use as integral to the understanding of meaning, and attributes to autonomy to the legal text, or to the legal lexicon which it establishes. As Jackson contends, Hart is unconcerned with the semiotic presuppositions of the communication of meaning. In short, hart sees no reason to go beyond the surface level of the way people actually think and talk about the law, and every reason not to do so. The actions of people, inspired by their intentions, are what count (Jackson, 1985).

Jackson divides Greimas's remark on legal semiotics into three parts with detailed analysis, namely, semantic, combinatorial and pragmatic part. In terms of the relation between semiotics and philosophy of law, the core idea of Jackson is that there is certain relation among semiotics, positivist jurisprudence, natural law theory and American positivist jurisprudence. Jackson thinks that it may not be able to reduce law to a single semiotic system, but people can characterize the various semiotic systems which claim to be legal and also analyze their inter-relationship. Such an endeavor would refine and advance Hart's programme in the following respect. It would endorse his rejection of the search for a definition of law. It would attend, rather, to questions of variety and inter-relationship. But it would conduct its investigation not at the level of the different linguistic uses of law, conceived as a concept, but rather at that of the discursive products and practices of different semiotic groups (Jackson, 1985). He also held the view that the consistency of the law is contradictory to the pluralistic objects used by different groups. Therefore, he makes a distinction of the semiotic discourse among the legislation, doctrine and judiciary, and considers the executive organ as the receivers of the legal information sent by the legislation organs.

Any such attempt to build up an overall semiotic mode of law must necessarily take positions on some basic theoretical issue: the status and identity of the referent and the minimal units of signification. Very different results will be obtained, depending upon the choices made on these issues (Jackson, 1985). The goal of that approach (legal theory based on the Greimasian Semiotics) is predominantly linguistic/analytic, and unfolds within the boundaries of legal theory, decidedly at distance to legal practices. The approach is, moreover, entirely multilingual, with English, French and German as the main players, not to mention Spanish and Italian. Be aware that not all contributions to the field are in English, and being not translated from, let us say Italian, into English is not a sign of depreciation. They furthermore refer most generally to the Civil Law and do not mention issues related to or exemplified by studies pertaining to the US or other Common Law systems (Broekman & Backer, 2013).

2. Legal Theory Based on the Peircean Semiotics

As far as Peirce is concerned, law, being similar to other social phenomena, such as language, economy, politics and family and so on, is a process of semiotic communication and information exchange carried out by the signs and the system of signs. As the symbolic argument, law is the prototype of daily language. The holistic concepts of the legal system, including the legal texts and communication process of legal implementation, function as the mode of dialectical thinking development. Related to economy and other systems, the legal whole is the prototype of the holistic social value exchange of the subjects. Each interpretation of the signs will generate new and more complicated signs with added meanings. The idea of constantly increased information in the semiotic process is the pivotal point in the Peircian methodology.

It is Peirce's main contribution to philosophical thought, he says in his final years, that a Method of Methods as he conceives it should be the method of semiotic inquiry, the aim of which is to be able to (1) account for various discipline-specific methods of investigation and (2) evolve from these diverse threads of discourse general principles of a unifying nature (Kevelson, 1987). Peirce still reckons that there is no ideal legal system but merely an extant sub-system network of law with mutual competition and conflicts. Legal system will never be a completely closed one and legal code will never be good once and for all. He provides a dialectical mode of reasoning to take the place of the closed thinking mode of syllogism, to show that there are definitely other choices even a judgment has been reached in a trial. This is the best method for interpreting the contradiction among the legal norms and the amendment of the original judgment. Certainly, this open mode of reasoning will generate further studies. Peirce considers his method as pragmatism or semiotics with the aim of applying the scientific method to philosophy. All in all, this method looks upon the law as a system of signs related with other social semiotic systems including language, economy and government etc. (Lv & Xu, 1991).

It is in the United States that Peircian influence has been most prominent. The legal theory of Peircian semiotics was rooted in Peircian pragmatism and logic, with its primary studies group headquartered in North America. In 1984, the Center for Semiotic Research in Law, Government and Economics was established in America and then the new International Association for Law and Semiotics was developed in next year. Peirce forms the focus for the entire work of Roberta Kevelson. Indeed, in much of it the law is seen as a means to exemplify, and sometimes to refine, the Peircian concepts themselves (Jackson, 2010). The magic of law has a name—the name is "language". Lawyers consider language as their precious instrument but mingle signs and words, fuse doctrine and expressiveness, mix names and symbols. Names, doctrines and other legal expressions are in Peirce's view a sign, a core concept of each process of meaning formation. A sign is for Peirce a something that relates to something else for someone in some respect or capacity (Broekman & Backer, 2013).

This approach riveted on the core concept, that is, sign, which is a nuclear concept or the pivotal technique for understanding meaning in law. The representatives of the legal theory based on Peircian semiotics includes Roberta Kevelson, Peter Goodrich, all considering law as a system of signs. As Roberta Kevelson argues, there are at least six major areas of concern at present in legal semiotics: (1) legal system considered as complex structure of signs and sign relationships; (2)the widely held assumption that legal codes are "mirrors" of society; (3) structure of legal reasoning, both according to syllogism and to what Peirce calls "dialogism"; (4) relations between logic, ethics, and value, the three parts of the normative sciences in general semiotic theory; (5) roles of fiction in legal procedure, both according to Bentham and as defined in current jurisprudential writings; (6)the conflict between Holmes's concept of law and the Austinian concept of law as command of the sovereign (Kevelson, 1988). Peirce forms the focus for the entire work of Roberta Kevelson. Indeed, in much of it the law is seen as a means to exemplify, and sometimes to refine, the Peircian concepts themselves. For Kevelson, law is seen as an entity which manifests Peircian claims about epistemology in general. Semiotics is here viewed as "a method of inquiry into the process of inquiry" and "assumes that inquiry, always dialogic, is a process of communication or message exchange by means of signs and sign systems". Kevelson regards law as "a prototype of intersubjective social exchange of value as a whole" (Kevelson, 1988).

As a holistic legal semiotics, there are some common characteristics among different scholars. In the first place, scholars of legal semiotics view the law as a semiotic system consisting of legal signs by applying the viewpoints and methods of semiotics to analyzing the legal phenomenon. They all deem semiotics as a meta-science, therefore the legal theory of semiotics, in essence, is still of a scientific one. In terms of research method, they are all in favor of positivism and give up the method of metaphysics. In this sense, legal semiotics is the reflection of western contemporary scientism in the jurisprudence. In the second place, scholars of legal semiotics look upon the law as a broad language phenomenon which is greatly influenced by the linguistic philosophy and in particular the school of daily linguistics. As it can be seen, there are linguistic nouns and terminologies in their theories, and they put emphasis on the analysis of the characteristics of legal languages and even attribute the law to the verbal conduct of the law. In the third place, scholars of legal semiotics highlight the studies achievements of positivist jurisprudence and widely extract the materials from both the American and Scandinavian positivist jurisprudence. Hence, both the dynamic and open ideas are emphasized in the jurisprudence, and the same is also the position and function of judge in the legal activities. What's more, this legal theory based on Peircian semiotics has also done particular exploration into such legal problems as the structure and function of the law, legal language, legal interpretation and legal control and so on.

It is worthy of notice that in addition to a variety of semiotic approached of law, scholars in American law have make tremendous contributions to the development of legal semiotics which enjoys the same position of the development of rhetoric studies being a closely related domain in the legal research sphere. An exemplary character of those scholarly exposés is, however, its inward-looking character and obsessed with the peculiar and temporally fashionable issues that interest the US legal academic establishment. Semiotically, one might be tempted to suggest that semiotic studies in the United States is itself systemically symbolic, and focused on academic status relationships within a small, closed circle. Obviously, this approach is predominantly monolingual: all studies, enrollments, texts, analyses are in the English language. As a consequence, North American semiotics is sometimes difficult to grasp for non-Anglo-American legal scholars, since they almost naturally refer to the US Common Law, without mentioning the simple fact that this legal system is not the only legal system in the world. That produces a danger of irrelevance; fortunately, one dissipated by some level of European and Asian interest in the U.S. sources of legal semiotics (Broekman & Backer, 2013).

1.4 The Characteristics of Legal Semiotics

The development of legal semiotics enjoys not so long history because the generation of semiotics began in 1950s and the application of semiotics to legal sphere only started from 1980s. With relatively less time of development, legal semiotics is still in its growing phase. We may say that there are altogether mainly two characteristics for the legal semiotics.

1. Being a New Method Rather than a Theory

Rather than being a complete theory of jurisprudence, legal semiotics is more of a new method for jurisprudence studies as Peirce raised the idea "method of methods". Up till the nineteenth century, jurisprudence studies had undergone much progress with different schools of studies continuously emerging. We can say that the views on the laws have become much more profound than ever before and it is also hard for the scholars to make progress to surpass the ever ones. With times going, the much diligent scholars of jurisprudence have to make innovation in their studies to promote the development of this discipline. As a result, they sought all kinds of new research methods to be applied to the legal sphere and various types of theories on jurisprudence simultaneously had been produced. An array of research methods from other disciplines such as sociology, statistics, psychology, hermeneutics, and rhetoric were adopted by the pragmatic Americans. Europeans, however, were not reluctant to fall behind and they also turned to find new methods and apply them to jurisprudence. Therefore, we can see that new research fields such as new analytical-positivist jurisprudence and linguistic jurisprudence came into being. Under this background, semiotics was applied to jurisprudence as legal phenomena, legal concepts, and legal theories are all the symbolic representation and even the activities such as legislation and judgment done by judges are the process of symbolic operation (Xu, 1998). In short, law itself is the symbolic system and the legal activity is the process of communication of legal information. And semiotics is also considered the meta-science which can be applied to interpret any disciplines. It is also repeatedly highlighted by the legal semiotics that the aim of it is not to study the truth of laws but to concern how the meaning of the laws is generated. To be a complete theory, the theory itself must embody its own theoretical premises, ontology and conclusion. However, legal semiotics has no independent theoretical structure. Admittedly, semiotics as a discipline has its own theory and structure, but when it is applied to jurisprudence, there is short of specific research objects and different scholars are now using their recognized semiotic methods to analyze legal phenomena. In terms of legal semiotics, it has not developed its own set of theories.

2. Devoting Much to Legal Interpretation Rather than Legal Doctrines

Considering from the studies of legal semiotics, it focuses more on the description of legal phenomena and devotes more to abstract interpretation than develops its own legal doctrines. As legal semiotics is more of a method than a theory, it has done much in legal interpretation rather than developed its own theoretical structure. What appeals to it is not the nature and function but the meaning of the law and how the meaning is generated, which is far from the legal practice. What's more, the method of semiotics used in jurisprudence seems to make the legal interpretation become more abstract. Scholars or students who engage in legal semiotics must first have a good mastery of the basic theory of semiotics. As semiotics is a kind of very complicated discipline related to other disciplines such as logic, rhetoric, linguistics, philosophy and literature etc., those who devote to this have to understand the complicated meaning of such terms as phoneme, syntax, text, argument, and jargon and so on. In this way, the scholars are making the interpretation more complex contrary to their aim of giving much clearer interpretation (Xu, 1998). Certainly, the objective to make the elite law popular among the public itself is not an easy task especially when you try to use the academic discourse.

1.5 Significance of Linguistic Turn of Western Jurisprudence

Compared with the distinct and clear legal theory, legal semiotics, admittedly, is more of pedantic and complex nature. In a sense, legal semiotics is also a game theory developed by European and American scholars. In spite of that, any methods or doctrines, as long as being developed after careful consideration, bear its own values. The linguistic turn of jurisprudence represents the breakthrough and innovation in the paradigm of jurists' theoretical studies. It also results from important intellectual resources from linguistics that is fitting with law research. The interdisciplinary and multi-dimensional studies paradigms have been skeptical of the legal linguistic views of traditional jurisprudence and tried to deconstruct and reconstruct it. It undermines the efforts to shape philosophy of law in the "grand theoretical narrative" underpinned by the essence of traditional jurisprudence that law is definitive, uniform and universal while trying to find constancy in the ever-changing phenomena. The paradigm of linguistic turn challenges the universal knowledge and theory of traditional jurisprudence. Meanwhile, a pluralistic and differentiated theory of legal knowledge is promoted and popularized. Within this paradigm, law is not considered as a set of principles and rules anymore. It symbolizes human communication and interpretation, narration, and ornamentation. Legal discourse, as a part of language, remains an idea, a cultural tradition, an integral part of culture, as well as its sign and symbol. The contextualism or locality of legal knowledge means that each of us must observe and understand the world based on his language, experience, and cultural environment. The contextualism or locality of knowledge inevitably leads to a legal concept characterized by anti-foundationalism. Law is not only a "language game" or a "lifestyle" but also a kind of local knowledge. Wherever and whenever we are, our knowledge is temporary, changing with experience. Legal knowledge is not an a priori proposition that transcends time and space, but something attached to a certain juridical practice. Contrary to the view that law is universal, law is not a bounded set of problems such as place, time, class, norms, rules, principles, [or] values, but also the sentimental aspect, things happened bearing the local characteristic and having relation with local people's manner of imagining the real (Geertz, 2000).

In short, the linguistic turn of jurisprudence holds revolutionary significance for the paradigm of jurisprudential studies, as it leads to a re-examination of language that was no longer treated as a tool, but as a philosophical afterthought in relation to the human being. First of all, it reveals the importance of studying the meaning of legal terminologies and concepts, which are the tools of legal thought and expression. Whether the legal thoughts and expressions are correct and effective or not is dependent on the extent of clear and rational expression of legal terms and concepts. Therefore, the study of legal concepts, especially the basic concepts, should be essential to philosophy of law. Secondly, it emphasizes linguistic awareness in law studies. When thinking of and expressing legal ideas, legal researchers must be aware of the correct use of language to ensure that the meaning of language is clear and consistent, thus avoiding the confusion of ideas caused by language obfuscation. Thirdly, it demonstrates a new method to studying legal concepts. Linguistic analysis is the process of identifying, selecting or defining the meaning of words and concepts by analyzing linguistic elements and structures and examining their origins, contexts and clues, rather than directly defining them in an abstract and arbitrary way (Huang, 2000).

This transformation of paradigm has breathed new life and vitality into law studies and has led to a truly postmodern turn. The traditional belief in the legal kingdom has been shattered, the legal discourse demystified and the relationship between legal practices and other practices unraveled. Thus, in the foreseeable future, such paradigm as "linguistic turn" will secure a more prominent place in legal studies. Noticeably, an interdisciplinary subject, namely, legal linguistics has come into being since the 1960s in European countries and America. In China, studies on the legal linguistics originally started from the end of 1970s, and it has not gained swift development until the 1990s. Once, nearly 5 types of related teaching materials or monographs appeared in 10 years. At the same time, the western related research and theory have also been brought into China which has given much enlightenment to Chinese Scholars with several established monographs emerging. Nowadays, legal linguistics has attracted scholars from three fields including jurisprudence, foreign language and Chinese to devote much in the academic studies of this field (Zou, 2020). According to Pan Qingyun's statistics, there are over 34 kinds of monographs on this subject having been published in recent 20 years (Pan, 2017). The lansign has noumenal status on the framework of "subject-object-subject" of contemporary philosophical epistemology. This epistemology (some scholars call it "general epistemology") is called epistemology of theory of language. The theoretical basis of legal linguistics is epistemology of theory of language, whose fundamental theory is ontology and the constructivism of legal language, and comparatively mature research methods are semantic analytical method and critical discourse analysis, etc. (Zou, 2020). As for the future development of Chinese forensic linguistics, Pan Qingyun puts forward four suggestions including further strengthening and stabilizing the team of studies, consolidating the basic theoretical studies in forensic linguistics, closely relating to the judicial practice and complying with comprehensively promoting law-based governance, and interacting with international counterparts of the same occupation, thereby promoting the healthy development of the international discipline with concerted efforts (Pan, 2017).

1.6 Conclusion

All in all, despite such emphasis having been done by western jurists and an interdisciplinary subject, legal linguistic, is also created, it is a pity that Chinese jurisprudence has generally not paid enough attention to this paradigm, let alone applying it in their research in law studies. In other words, the semiotic analysis is currently of little application in the law practice. It is attributed to the lack of academic literacy, and more related to the methodological flaw, that is, the neglect of the paradigm of semantic analysis of the linguistic turn. It can be argued that "in contemporary Chinese, law studies on concepts and categories and even in major law debates are met with opposing views. … The origin and focus of the debate are often caused by the ambiguity of concepts and categories". However, "some arguments can be avoided or resolved if both parties involved in the discussion are good at using semantic analysis to identify the linguistic difference between the same words, concepts and propositions …" (Zhang, 1996). This surely requires law scholars to experience a linguistic turn of semantic analysis in the paradigm. On the one hand, they need to examine the language, its context and the meanings it carries and the information it contains. On the other hand, they should engage themselves in interdisciplinary discussions covering multiple linguistic domains to enjoy the diversity of the world. After all, "jurisprudence has a range of bilateral and multilateral problems with other disciplines. Hence, it needs to communicate, have dialogue and cooperate with philosophy, history, economics, politics, sociology, ethics, logic, behavioral science and other disciplines" (Zhang, 1996). The linguistic turn of western jurisprudence shows once again that legal studies must not only stand on its own stance and be interpreted or defended by the legal profession themselves. It is necessary to draw on the experience from and travel across multiple domains of discourse and linguistic spaces that is incommensurable. Therefore, the future of law studies will definitely be "a debate across multiple, incommensurable fields of discourse and multiple linguistic games" (Ryuichi, 2000), rather than anything else.

References

Broekman, J. M., & Backer, L. C. (2013). *Lawyers making meaning*. Springer Science & Business Media.

Chang, A., & Zhu, M. (2003). "Linguistics diversion of law" and its inspiration to methodology of law linguistics research in our country. *Journal of Qiongzhou University, 3*, 63–68.

Dong, X. (2006). Law and language: The transformation of approaches to the study of western legal language. *Social Science Front, 2*, 205–209.

Du, Y., & Zhang, W. (2001). The postmodern method and the turn of the study of law. *Jilin University Journal Social Sciences Edition, 3*, 30–36.

Gadamer, H. G. (1976). *Philosophical hermeneutics*. University of California Press.

Gadamer, H. G. (1999). *Truth and method* (H. Hong, Trans.). Shanghai Translation Publishing House.

Geertz, C. (2000). *Local knowledge* (H. Wang & J. Zhang, Trans.). Central Compilation & Translation Press.

Guo, W. (2012). Marriage to the law: The correspondence of the method of semiotics and jurisprudence and its scope. *Journal of Henan Judicial Police Vocational College, 1*, 88–94.

Guo, W., & Zou, X. (2012). The correspondence of method of semiotics and jurisprudence and its application. *HuBei Social Sciences, 4*, 155–159.

Hu, Y. (2005). A review of methodologies of the three major schools of western jurisprudence. *Journal of Comparative Law, 2*, 20–32.

Huang, W. (2000). Explanation of the philosophy of law. *Chinese Journal of Law, 5*, 3–16.

Jackson, B. S. (1985). *Semiotics and legal theory*. Routledge & Kegan Paul.

Jackson, B. S. (2010). Legal semiotics and semiotic aspects of jurisprudence.

Kevelson, R. (1987). *Law and semiotics* (Vol. 1). Plenum Press.

Kevelson, R. (1988). *The law as a system of signs*. Plenum Press.

Li, Q. (2005). *Law research and methodology*. Shandong People's Publishing House.

Lv, S. (1999). *Schools of the modern western jurisprudence* (Vol. I). Encyclopedia of China Publishing House.

Lv, S., & Xu, A. (1991). Review on the western legal theory of semiotics. *Jiangsu Social Science, 5*, 41–45.

Niu, Y. (2015). *Law and semiotics interpretation*. Doctoral dissertation, Nanjing University.

Pan, Q. (2017). *Forensic linguistics*. China University of Political Science and Law Press.

Ryuichi, N. (2000). On the shift of in paradigm jurisprudence studies in the 20th century (Y. Zhou, Trans.). *Global Law Review, 3*, 13–27.

Shen, Z. (1983). Chaim Perelman's legal thought on the new rhetoric. *Chinese Journal of Law, 5*, 75–80.

Shu, G. (1995). The development of German philosophy of law in the postwar period. *Journal of Comparative Law, 4*, 227–355.

Wagner, A., & Broekman, J. M. *Prospects of legal semiotics*. Springer.

Wang, J. (2001). *Legal translation between the east and west: A study of the introduction of western law in nineteenth century China*. China University of Political Science and Law Press.

Xie, H. (2003). Science and interpretation: Two logical thoughts of studying legal philosophy. *Science of Law (Journal of Northwest University of Political Science and Law), 1*, 3–14.

Xu, A. (1998). Several aspects of European structuralist semiotic jurisprudence. *Peking University Law Journal, 4*, 118–123.

Zhang, W. (1996). *Study on the western thoughts of the legal philosophies in the 20th century*. Law Press China.
Zheng, Q. (2000). An overview of postmodern jurisprudence in America. *Global Law Review, 2*, 44–53.
Zou, Y. (2020). Re-thinking on theory and method of legal linguistics. *Journal of Beihua University, 5*, 1–7.

Chapter 2
Language and Law

2.1 Legal Language

Legal Language does not qualify as a language in the same way as Chinese, English or French. Originated in the west, the term "legal language" refers to the language or part of a specific language used for expressing legal concepts and dealing with litigation and non-litigation legal affairs. Later, the connotation of this term extents to those words and expressions possessing certain legal significance, bring the term to another linguistic level. Like financial language, advertising language, and scientific language, legal language is also a language for special purposes. In general, legal language is a formalized language based on logic rules which differs from the ordinary natural language in vocabulary, morphology, syntax, and semantics, as well as other linguistic features (Wydick et al., 2005).

Obviously, legal language is based on ordinary language. For that reason, the grammar and the vocabulary of legal language are generally the same as those of the ordinary language. However, legal language is a language for special purposes. This means, first of all, there are a large number of legal terms containing unique properties as per branch of law. In addition, legal languages of different countries and in different times possess different characteristics that distinguish them from ordinary written language. One may speak of a specific legal style. Therefore, for the general public, it may be a little difficult to comprehend the accurate meaning of legal language. As Tiersma (1999) points out, "Legal language has been called an argot, a dialect, a register, a style, and even a separate language. In fact, it is best described with the relatively new term sublanguage. A sublanguage has its own specialized grammar and allows 'deviant' rules of grammar that are not acceptable in the standard language. However, we describe it, legal language is a complex collection of linguistic habits that have developed over many centuries and that lawyers have learned to use quite strategically".

Legal language is often characterized as a technical language, that is, a language used by professionals. There is some truth to this position. Legal language is generally used by lawyers and judges. Nevertheless, when members of the lay public are

X. Dong and Y. Zhang, *Chinese Legal Translation and Language Planning in the New Era*, https://doi.org/10.1007/978-981-19-8448-8_2

involved as parties, experts, or jurors, they will inevitably be confronted with legal language, which in many cases will create a need for some kind of explanation or translation (as when jury instructions try to explain legal concepts in ordinary language). In the meanwhile, it seems natural to say that a citizen who, for example, writes his own will following a model form is use legal language. More importantly, in contrast with other languages for special purposes, the target of messages transmitted in legal language often covers the overall public, certain class of the public or a number of particular citizens. For example, a law normally requires compliance by all members of the society while a court judgement relates only to the specific parties involved in the case so tried. Thus, legal language is not an instrument aimed solely at internal communication within the legal profession.

The use of legal language is widespread and of great significance since it governs all areas and aspects of social life and can, through intertextuality, be combined with languages of different domains. Additionally, legal language has a long historical standing, which is not necessarily the case with most other languages for special purposes. This is why legal language have shaped the ordinary language of various countries and regions in a significant manner. And the great influences of legal language on ordinary language continues up to now.

Legal language nowadays can be understood both in a narrow sense and a broad sense. In a narrow sense, legal language merely refers to legislative language used in normative documents. In a broad sense, legal language refers to legislative, executive, and judicial language. As for legislative language, it generally refers to the formal and concrete language used in the legal provisions, such as the Constitution of a State, civil law, criminal law, regulations and other normative pronouncements which permit, command, or prohibit a certain caused of conduct. As for executive language, it is normally defined as the language used in the process of implementing the law, such as in the process of detention. As for judicial language, it, as the name implies, is the language employed in the courtroom, such as judicial decisions, briefs, appeals, petitions and remarks by judges, lawyers, witnesses, and other participants, whether in written or oral form. For example, the spoken judicial language may include the language used by lawyers in courtroom disputes, and speeches delivered by the plaintiffs, defendants, judges and otherwise.

In this chapter, we will basically focus on the legislative language since it is mainly embodied in the written form, which is more compact and denser, while the executive language and judicial language involve spoken forms, which tends to be less formal. Besides, the legislative language is the most representative among the three categories of legal language aforementioned.

2.2 Linguistic Features of Legal Language

The law and language are inseparable. "in all societies, law is formulated, interpreted, and enforced… and the greater part of these different legal process is realized primarily through language. Language is the medium, process and product in the various arenas of the law where legal texts, spoken or written, are generated in the service of regulating behavior" (Maley, 1994). The close relationship between law and language has endowed the law with distinct linguistic features. These features are, to some extent, common in all legal languages (for example, Chinese, English, French). The following is an overview of the principal linguistic features of legal language.

1. Precision and Fuzziness

Precision and accuracy are regarded as fundamental features of legal language. The inherent seriousness of legal language makes it essential to avoid all inaccurate and unclear expressions as inaccuracy would lead to ambiguity and ambiguity would lead to misunderstanding, and further to dispute. To avert the risk of arbitrariness, legal rules should be formulated as precise as possible. Therefore, accuracy and precision can be called the soul of legal language and linguistic clarity is the inexorable law of legislation.

The basic goal of legal language is to transmit legal messages with absolute clarity. This essentially results from the requirement for legal protection and legal certainty. Hence, legislators are required to make a detailed distinction among words that are interchangeably used by layman. For example, the differences between "right and privilege", "duty and obligation", "jail and prison", and "residence and domicile", may be of little consequence in daily communication, but extremely significant in legal contexts. Only when accurate and precise expressions are adopted in legal language, can legislation provide people with behavioral mode or standard and then the goal of "rule of law" be realized.

However, fuzziness is also a prominent feature of legal language. It is universally acknowledged that no matter how hard we try, it is difficult to express all specific behavioral modes, motivations, and results in a successful and comprehensive manner just with the limited language symbols. The fact is that fuzziness comes into being inevitably when language is applied to carry an array of information. Legal language, as a part of natural language, is also intrinsically fuzzy.

Fuzzy expressions are usually employed in the legal texts in order to improve the generality of the language, so as to enumerate different situations to the largest extent, for example, to settle the case that has never happened before, or that we cannot foresee. With respect to international relations, linguistic fuzziness may also be a conscious choice in certain negotiating situations. For example, negotiators can leave equivocal an article of an international treaty on which they have not reached any agreement. To achieve generality and flexibility, legal language usually adopts words like "acceptable" and "reasonable" for the purpose of realizing effective communicative function and a term like "appropriate" can change with times and circumstances. However, a fuzzy word or expression would leave plenty of room for interpretation and thus give great discretion to the judges in the decision-making process. Therefore, generality and flexibility are necessary but should be limited in use since people should know in advance what can be done and what cannot. In brief, the relationship between the two features of legal language, namely, precision and fuzziness, is not contradictory but complementary, thus making the legal system comprehensive and complete.

2. Information Overload

In a modern and highly complicated society, the number of legal rules can hardly be figured out. The numerous legal rules aptly sum up the situation. To help stem the tide, legal language should be as concise as possible, otherwise the laws and regulations would be tediously long and unclear in meaning. In the meanwhile, legal language should avoid over-abstraction, in that way enabling decoding with minimum effort.

Harmonizing these goals is not easy. The key is to figure out for whom the laws are formulated: experts or the general public? Even laws concerning fundamental questions of citizens' lives are often formulated for experts since they are charged with the technical application of such laws. A typical example may be affairs of social and fiscal law. With respect to these affairs, laws are necessarily of high complexity: this is a matter of distributive justice, which presuppose highly detailed rules. These rules might even express in language from a mathematical formula relating to the calculation of some welfare allowance or a tax to be paid. This means that social and fiscal laws should be formulated in a compacted manner, with as high a density of information as possible, in order to prevent meaningless lengthiness.

The legislator does not suppose that law of a technical character is understandable form the standpoint of general public. As we have seen, the principles of these laws are communicated to citizens by means of short-form bulletins, leaving out the details. It is easy to understand the problem caused by the great density of information of legal language concerns not only legislative language. In many civil-law countries like France, the language of judgement is traditionally loaded with messages: it is compact and full of expressions that have the appearance of abridged codes. Today, following criticisms from linguists, judgements in some countries are written in a language closer to ordinary language. However, some scholars have commented that this means, on one hand, that judgements have become too long, and on the other hand, weakens their internal logic: a judgement formulated in ordinary language contains more secondary, even meaningless, elements, impeding transmission of the subject legal messages.

3. Neutrality

In general, legal language today tends to be official and formal. The style of this type of language is as neutral as possible as the main intention is to influence the understanding instead of feeling of the readers or listeners. This is why an author argued that the style of legal language is "cold": it rejects all that is affective and dose not include emotional elements. This is why legal texts contain practically no exclamation or question marks. Nor should legal language give rise to irrelevant associations that distract the attention of the reader of the document or discourse in question. The neutrality of legal language is largely guaranteed by the fact that many legal texts (for example, laws, administrative instructions, judgements) pass through the offices of several commentators and stylists before receiving their final form: they are not from a single hand.

The rigorousness of the requirement for linguistic neutrality varies according to the general cultural and traditions of the country in question. In civil-law countries, it is self-evident that a judge should express himself in an absolutely calm and composed way. On this topic, it appears that Anglo-American judges enjoy a far greater freedom. An illustration of this is the dissenting opinion of Judge Musmanno of the Pennsylvania Supreme Court in the case relating to Henry Miller's work, "Tropic of Cancer" (Tiersma, 1999): "'Cancer' is not a book. It is a cesspool, an open sewer, a pit of petrification, a slimy gathering of all that is rotten in the debris of human depravity. And in the center of all this waste and stench, besmearing himself with its foulest defilement, splashes, leaps, cavorts and wallows a bifurcated specimen that responds to the name of Henry Miller… From Pittsburg to Philadelphia, from Dan to Beersheba, and from Ramparts of *the Bible* to Samuel Eliot Morison's *Oxford History of the American People*, I dissent".

4. Objectivization and Impersonality

As a frozen style, the legal language manifests its authoritativeness and solemness by employing objective and impersonal expressions. This feature is best proved by the frequent use of the "impersonal construction" which means the avoidance of the first and second personal pronouns like "I" and "you" (Tiersma, 1999). For instance, Article 46 of Criminal Law provides that "Any criminal who is sentenced to fixed-term imprisonment of life imprisonment shall serve his sentence in prison or another place for the execution". The usage of third person pronouns gives an objective impression to the public and guarantees the act in practice that the cases are decided in accordance with the legislative authority instead of personal emotions. Other linguistic devices contributing to the objectivity include the passive voice, which is also noticeably used in legal documents. This brings the object of the action into the foreground, giving the actor only a secondary role. This feature is prominent in all specialist languages. In this way, authors of legal texts underline the objectivity of their findings and conclusions.

Both "impersonal constructions" and passive voice create and impression of objectivity and strengthen the authority of law. To sum up, the feature of being objective and impersonal reflects the essence of law, that is, to judge every case only by rule of law rather than the rule of man.

5. Sentence Complexity and Diversity of Language Elements

Sentences in legal language are generally very long and complicated. This is largely due to force of tradition since legal language involves a language for special purposes of great antiquity whose stylistic elements often stem from Medieval Latin. Even in our times, complicated and useless expressions are added to legal texts, making them more difficult to understand. For instance, in the United States, there is a fondness for using expressions considered "polished" and "energetic" (Tiersma, 1999): *at slow speed* instead of *slowly, in the event that* instead of *if, prior to* instead of *before, subsequent to* instead of *after*.

Difficulties of understanding also occur because legal and administrative language places less emphasis on verbs than ordinary language. This is partly explained by the notion according to which a noun gives a more objective impression than a verb, notably in cases involving findings of fact. The wealth of nouns in legal and administrative texts is accentuated by the fact that these nouns often form phrases (groups of words forming a lexical unit) or notably in some languages, such as German, the Scandinavian languages and so on. This is because a term created to express a new legal concept should also be as transparent as possible, this is, it immediately shows the uninitiated what it is about. If the particular words forming part of the phrase or compound word in question each express an essential feature of the new concept, then such transparency is ensured. For example, *contrat de transfert de processus technologique, Cour de justice des Commuautes europeennes* in French or *Ausagevenveigerungsrecht, Klageerzwingungsverfahren* in German. These examples show the price of transparency: expressions in legal language are often complicated.

Further, different language elements mingle in legal language. Firstly, this language contains words and expressions from ordinary language and adopts the ordinary meaning thereof. Secondly, legal language contains words and expressions from ordinary language but adopts the technical meaning. Thirdly, legal language contains words and expressions that are purely technical terms. These may be legal terms or terms from any other professional domain. Linguistic research affirms that, in legal texts, the number of such legal terms with pure legal connotation is relatively limited in comparison with other languages for special purposes. The majority of legal terms are words and expressions from ordinary language having particular meaning in legal contexts. This is sometimes dangerous: the uninitiated reader imagines having understood the meaning of the term, but the term actually means something else in legal language.

Additionally, legal texts always contain terms from other professional domain (for example, technology, economics). A typical example may be texts produced by organs of European Union. A directive of the European Communities on agriculture may include terms from law, agronomy, commerce, and technology. An in-depth understanding of such a directive requires knowledge of all these domains, which further deepens the hermetic character of the text.

2.3 Legal Texts

1. Classification of Legal Texts

Legal texts can be classified pursuant to different criteria. For instance, Jean-Claude Gemar, divides legal texts into three groups according to the subject-matter, such as whether the text regulates public or private affairs. The first group of texts contains laws, regulations, judgements, and international treaties; the second group contains contracts, administrative and commercial forms, wills, and otherwise; and the third group contains scholarly works (Sacevic, 1997). One major problem with this classification is that many documents employed in the legal process and translated as such are excluded from classification, for example, documents used in court proceedings.

As a type of special-purpose texts, legal texts can also be classified by functions. In legal theory, the most widely accepted classification is the bipartite system in which language have two major functions: regulatory function and informative function, for example, prescriptive function and descriptive function (Sacevic, 1997). The regulatory legal texts generally possess a prescriptive function and typical examples of this group include laws, regulations, codes, contracts, treaties, and conventions. Such texts are normative instruments containing rules of conduct or norms. On the other hand, the informative legal texts normally consist of hybrid texts that are primarily descriptive but also contain certain prescriptive properties. This group of legal texts includes judicial decisions and legal instruments that are used in judicial and administrative proceedings such as actions, pleading, briefs, appeals, requests, petitions, and otherwise (Li & Zhang, 2006).

Accordingly, legal texts may have various communicative purposes. They can serve a normative purpose as in the case of laws, statutes and other documents that establish legal facts or create rights and obligations. Most of the legal texts show a strong prescriptive character. Legal texts can also serve an informative purpose as in some legal scholarly works and commentaries, legal advice, correspondence between layers, and documents used in court proceedings. These are, to the largest extent, descriptive. For legal translators, it is necessary to ascertain the legal status and communicative purpose of the original texts and target texts as these may have impact on translation. For example, the main characteristics of a law can be described as authority and formality, but those of a testimony may be reliability and facticity. This section deals primarily with normative texts like statues, codes, treaties and international conventions.

2. Tone of Legal Texts

As is known to all, legal texts are formulated in a professional language generally known as the language of law. Legislative writing is so impersonal that it is independent of whoever the drafter is or the addressee is. The general function of legal texts is regulatory and informative, or to impose obligations and to confer rights. In translation, the tone of a text is the key to its communicative effectiveness and has to be determined by the translators. Therefore, keeping the tone of legal texts in mind does help translators understanding the importance of the function of legal texts in translation.

The function of legal texts plays a crucial role in determining translation strategy and achieving the desired legal effects. It is believed that the correct understanding of legal texts is not only the basis on which the legal translators grasp the intention and the function of legal text concerned but also the decisive factor to determine the translation strategy, methods and skills to be adopted.

(1) Commands and Requirements

A legal command imposes a duty upon the legal subject to act in a certain manner under given circumstances. Legal commands are mandatory provisions, thus failing to act accordingly constitutes a violation of law punishable. The English practice of imposing legal duties by the legal imperative *shall* is a longstanding practice dating backing to English transition of Roman law texts. The first extant translation of *Magna Carta*, originally in Latin, has been called "an exercise in *shall*".

Example 1: 税务机关依照前款规定作出纳税调整, 需要补征税款的, 应当补征税款, 并依法加收利息。

Translation: Where tax authorities make tax payment adjustments under the preceding paragraph, which requires collection of taxes in arrears, such taxes in arrears shall be collected, together with interest thereon in accordance with the law.

Example 2: 居民个人向扣缴义务人提供专项附加扣除信息的, 扣缴义务人按月预扣缴税款时应当按照规定予以扣除, 不得拒绝。

Translation: Where a resident individually provides the withholding agent with information on special additional deductibles, the withholding agent shall, when withholding and prepaying taxes on a monthly basis, make deductions as required, and shall not refuse to do so.

(2) Permission and Authorization

In addition to imposing duties, legislative texts also confer rights, privileges, and powers on legal subjects in the form of permission and authorization. The modal *may* is usually used to express permission and authorization in English. While it is agreed that a permission expresses a facultative operation, there are cases where the courts have interpreted a permissive *may* as *shall*, thus turning it into a mandatory provision. Although authorization can be construed as a duty, such provisions are usually fuzzy as to whether the performance of an authorized act is mandatory.

As for permission, lawyers often say that an act that is not expressively prohibited is permitted. Yet there are a number of explicit permissions. By granting permission, the legislatures limit the number of potential prohibitions. More importantly, the granting of a permission represents a way of cancelling certain command, requirement, or prohibition, or making an exception to certain command, requirement, or prohibition.

As for authorization, it is a special type of legal speech act in which the permissive *may, shall, have the right/power to, enjoy the right of, be entitled/empowered to, be authorized to,* etc. and Chinese expressions "享有……权利", "有权……" can be construed as expressing a right. Technically speaking, authorizations confer power upon some person or authority to perform an act which otherwise that person or authority would be without power to perform.

Example 1: 交通主管部门、公路管理机构负有管理和保护公路的责任, 有权检查、制止各种侵占、损坏公路、公路用地、公路附属设施及其他违反本法规定的行为。

Translation: Departments in charge of transportation and highway administration organizations are responsible for the administration and protection of the roads and are empowered to check and stop all acts that occupy, damage roads, land used by roads, and road ancillary facilities and other acts that violate provisions of this Law.

Example 2: 各民族公民都有用本民族语言、文字进行民事诉讼的权利

Translation: Citizens of all ethnicities shall be entitled to use their native spoken and written languages in civil procedures.

(3) Prohibitions

Prohibitions are legal speech acts with the illocutionary force of forbidding. The most common type of prohibitions are acts that an individual or unit is explicitly forbidden to perform and whose performance is punishable. In view of their obligatory nature, such prohibitions are regarded as negative commands: X is obliged to refrain from performing act A; if X performs act A, then X is subject to punishment. As the very opposite of commands, prohibitions are expressed in English with the negation *shall/may/must not, be prohibited/not allowed, be not obliged/permitted* and in Chinese with "严禁", "禁止", "不得", etc.

Example 1: 证券的发行、交易活动, 必须遵守法律、行政法规; 禁止欺诈、内幕交易和操纵证券市场的行为。

Translation: The issuance and trading of securities shall abide by laws and administrative regulations. Any fraud, insider trading or manipulation of the securities market shall be prohibited.

Example 2: 国家建立健全旅游服务标准和市场规则, 禁止行业垄断和地区垄断。旅游经营者应当诚信经营, 公平竞争, 承担社会责任, 为旅游者提供安全、健康、卫生、方便的旅游服务。

Translation: The state shall establish and improve tourism service standards and market rules and prohibit industrial monopoly. Tourism operators shall operate in good faith, make fair competition, undertake social responsibilities, and provide safe, healthy, hygienic and convenient tourism services for tourists.

3. Translation of Legal Texts

As stated above, a legal text is vested with legal effects and intended to serve a specific function. For the most part, modern translation theorists no longer regard translation as a mechanical process of transcoding one language into another. Nor is a text regarded as "a string of words and structures to be converted into a string of equivalents" (Snell-Hornby, 1988). Primarily under the influence of German scholars, the main emphasis in general translation theory has shifted from language to the cultural aspects of translation.

Legal translation involves the transfer of a message from a legal text producer to a receiver. Lawyers are aware that, in order for plurilingual communication to be effective in the law, one must preserve the unity of the single instrument, as it is called in international law (Tabory, 1980). In other words, legal communication can be successful only if the legal translator is able to translate the message into linguistic code that is identical in meaning. Thus, legal translation is largely regarded as a means of transferring meaning by linguistic transcoding. This has long been recognized that the goal of legal translation is to preserve the meaning of the original texts, which consists in reproducing, transferring, or reconstructing the meaning of the source text as accurately as possible.

Unlike other special-purpose texts, the meaning of legal texts is usually dependent on local context, which is synonymous with legal context. It is in legal system that the texts are to be interpreted rather than the language itself. For instance, contracts are interpreted in accordance with law governing contractual affairs regardless of the language in which they are written. Accordingly, if a contract is governed by American law, the translation version of that contract will be interpreted according to American law. If a contract contains elements of foreign law, those elements may be interpreted according to foreign law in some cases.

Since the meaning of legal texts is determined mainly by legal context, lawyers admit that the presumption of the equal meaning can rarely be achieved in practice. Therefore, the main goal of legal translation cannot be producing a text with the same meaning as the source text. Legal translation is "an act of communication in the mechanism of law" instead of "a process of linguistic transcoding" (Sacevic, 1997). Hence, the source texts and the target texts must have the same communicative function. This brings us to the second presumption of legal translation, that is, the presumption of equal effects. The main task of legal translators is to produce a text that will lead to the same legal effects in practice. To produce such a text, they must understand not only what the words mean and what a sentence means, but also what legal effect it is supposed to have, and how to achieve that legal effect in the other language.

In a word, the goal of legal translation can be defined as to produce a text that is equal in meaning and effect with the source texts, whereby the main emphasis is on effect. That is to say, the target texts will be interpreted and applied by the courts in the same manner as the source texts. This is known as uniform interpretation and application (Sacevic, 1997). To this end, legal translators must produce a text that has the same communicative function as the source text. This is undoubtedly the most serious matter to be considered by legal translators in their decision-making process.

References

Li, K., & Zhang, X. (2006). *Legal texts and legal translation*. China Translation & Publishing Corporation.

Maley, Y. (1994). The language of the law. In J. Gibbons (Ed.), *Language and the law* (Vol. 11). Longman.

Mellinkoff, D. (1990). *The language of the law*. Little, Brow and Company.

Sacevic, S. (1997). *New approach to legal translation*. Kluwer Law International.

Snell-Hornby, M. (1988). *Translation studies, an integrated approach*. Benjamins.

Tabory, M. (1980). *Multilingualism in international law and institutions*. Sijthoff &Noordoff.

Tiersma, P. (1999). *Legal language*. The University of Chicago Press.

Wydick, R. C., et al. (2005). *California legal ethics*. West Publishing Company.

Chapter 3
Chinese Legal System

3.1 Introduction

A nation's development and rejuvenation call for not only strong economic power, but also profound cultural heritage. As a decisive factor for the formation of national spirit, culture exerts such significant influence on a nation's development to the extent the destiny thereof can be changed. For over 2000 years, the Chinese legal system, as an important part of traditional Chinese culture, has functioned as a powerful tool for protecting national unity and stability, maintaining social order, and promoting cultural communication. Even for now, in the transformation of modern Chinese society, the Chinese legal system also plays an irreplaceable role in constructing a socialist country under the rule of law and enriching the system of socialist rule of law with Chinese characteristics.

During the formation and development of the Chinese legal system, government of each dynasty have promulgated its own laws and regulations and politicians, philosophers, legal scholars and historians have written a great number of essays, articles and books to express their theories concerning law, justice and national governance, leaving us abundant legal classics. These traditional Chinese legal classics have stood the test of time, offering the world with such inspiring and everlasting ideas and arguments concerning law and national governance as "people being the foundation of the state", "combination of etiquette and laws", "the law does not favor the rich and powerful" and otherwise. According to *the Decision of the CPC Central Committee on Major Issues Pertaining to Comprehensively Promoting the Rule of Law* passed at the fourth plenary session of the 18th central committee of the communist party of China on October 23, 2014, the construction of a socialist country under the rule of law must be proceeded from China's reality. While drawing on other countries' useful experiences concerning the rule of law, the quintessence of traditional legal culture shall also be re-evaluated, appreciated and absorbed, since indiscriminate copy of others' concepts and modes of the rule of law can never bring us any satisfactory outcome (Xi, 2014).

X. Dong and Y. Zhang, *Chinese Legal Translation and Language Planning in the New Era*, https://doi.org/10.1007/978-981-19-8448-8_3

In the same year, President Xi Jinping, at the Symposium on Literary and Art Work, pointed out that there is a growing interest in China among the international community. People from other countries and regions are eager to know what kind of country China is, how Chinese people think of world, life and moral values, as well as what historical heritage, customs and habits, ethical characteristics do Chinese nation have… literary and art workers shall promote our excellent cultural works to the world, show the charm of Chinese culture to the foreign people and deepen their appreciation and understanding thereof (Xi, 2014). Since the 18th National Congress of the CPC, cultural diplomacy has become a concern for the overall diplomatic strategy in China and President Xi has referred to "cultural confidence" in multiple momentous occasions, with a view to advancing the progress of traditional Chinese culture. As stated in the report delivered at the 19th National Congress of the CPC, since socialism with Chinese characteristics has entered a new era, "we will improve our capacity for engaging in international communication so as to tell China's stories well, present a true, multi-dimensional, and panoramic view of China, and enhance our country's cultural soft power" (Xi, 2017).

3.2 The Chinese Legal System and the World's Legal Systems

In nature, the laws and legal cultures of different countries and regions show some similarities and universality and, in the meanwhile, are bound to have some unique characteristics respectively. Based on such similarities and differences, legal system can be referred to as the basic form of global legal culture ecosystem. Speaking of legal system, Hozumi Nobushige, one of the greatest jurists in modern Japan history, was the first one to propose this concept. In an essay entitled "*On Five Major Legal Systems*" published on the *Journal of Law Association* in 1884, he adopted terms in biosystematics and anthropology to compare and analyze the legal traditions and commonness of different legal cultures around the world and then categorized them into five major legal systems, which are "Indian legal system, Chinese legal system, Islamic legal system, English legal system and Roman legal system", inspiring legal scholars and researchers to make comparison among different laws and legal cultures, categorize them in a way a biological specie is categorized, and therefore establish the genealogy of law (Zhang, 2007a, 2007b). Later, John H. Wigmore, in *A Panorama of the World's Legal Systems* published in 1928, classified world legal systems into 16 major kinds in chronological order. As stated in the book, there are Egyptian legal system, Mesopotamian legal system, Chinese legal system, Hindu legal system, Hebrew legal system, Greek legal system, maritime legal system, Roman legal system, Celtic legal system, Germanic legal system, canon legal system, Japanese legal system, Islam legal system, Slavic legal system, civil law system, and common law system, among which the Chinese legal system is the third oldest legal system in the world, as well as the one that has continued to function as an effective mean of national governance for the longest period of time, that is, over 2000 years (Wigmore, 1928). In 1950, Rene David, French comparative jurist, argued in *Traite Elememtaire De Droit Civil Compare* that, on basis of different ideologies and legal techniques, legal systems in the world shall be classified as Western legal system, socialist legal system, Islam legal system, Indian legal system, and Chinese legal system (Huang, 2012). Many jurists have offered their own classifications regarding legal systems by all kinds of research methods and standards, but no matter how they approach this task, the Chinese legal system is indeed an integral part of the overall world legal systems that can never be overlooked.

To form a relatively complete legal system, three essential conditions must be satisfied. First of all, there should be a parent country, where the laws and institutions lay the legislative foundation for other member countries. In history, such East and South-East countries as Korea, Japan, and Vietnam have all been the dependent states of China, these countries have transplanted and localized Chinese laws and institutions to establish their own legal framework. As stated in *History of Korea*, "the overall institution of Korea was merely an imitation of that of Tang, the laws and regulations of which were also adopted to deal with all kinds of criminal conducts" (Jeong, 2014). Secondly, all countries under a legal system shall share the same legal traditions and have consistent legal institutions. The Chinese legal system has influenced each and every state and region in the "Confucian cultural circle". For example, in 701 AD, Emperor Mommu promulgated the *Taiho Code*, the first statutory code in the history of Japan, which is formulated exactly based on Tang Code (Ma & Shi, 2012). In fact, from 6 to 12th Century, due to frequent exchanges between Japan and China, Chinese laws along with its legal traditions and spirits were fully absorbed and transplanted by Japan. Thirdly, all countries under the legal system, though having a lot in common, should still have their own legal culture individuality. One necessary step that each of the member states under Chinese legal system would take after transplanting laws and institutions of China is localization, with a view to making the legal framework so constructed more suitable for their actual national conditions. Therefore, Chinese legal system is undoubtedly a complete legal system with magnificent historical influences.

It is generally recognized in domestic academic circles that Chinese legal system "mainly refers to the system of laws and institutions in the feudal China" (Zhang, 1984). As early as in the 407 BC, Li Kui, the great reformer in the State of Wei during the Warring States Period, formulated and promulgated *Fa Jing* (also called *The Book of Law*), the first systematic statutory code in the history of China, laying the foundation for Chinese legal system as it set a precedent for the following legislators from the such perspectives as legislative spirit, legislative framework and model, structure and form of code, legislative technique and otherwise. In 1740, the government of Qing dynasty, after more than 100 years of hard work and repeated amendments, complied and enacted the *Ta Tsing Leu Lee* (namely, the Great Qing Legal Code). It is the last but most comprehensive feudal code in Chinese history, epitomizing the overall traditional legal thoughts and legislation experiences. In a word, the development of Chinese legal system can be summarized as "sprouted in pre-Qin period, thrived in Sui and Tang dynasty, matured in Ming and Qing dynasty and collapsed in the late Qing dynasty" (Qiao, 1986), the history of which has not been interrupted for thousands of years, forming an integrated and independent legal system with distinct national features.

3.3 Characteristics of Chinese Legal System

1. Under Profound Influence of Confucianism

The Confucianism is the guiding ideology of Chinese legal system. With respect to the views on the universe or the world, Chinese legal system follows the principle of "unity of man and nature" and pursues the harmony between human and nature, human and society, as well as nature and society. The "nature" herein shall refer to the natural world in a cultural dimension, that is, an imprimitive world where human beings live. The Confucianists believe that human and nature are somehow interlinked, and we can find basis of law regulating human beings in the laws of nature. Anyone violating law will violate the laws of nature and is bound to be punished. So, every member in the society should revere the nature and obey the laws, therefore forming the harmony-oriented legal spirit.

With respect to national governance, the Confucianism advocates the combination of propriety and law. Both are pivotal code of conduct, as well as powerful means of social administration. In the Analects of Confucius, there is a saying "Lead the people with administrative injunctions (zheng 政) and keep them orderly with penal law (xing 刑), and they will avoid punishments but will be without a sense of shame. Lead them with excellence (de 德) and keep them orderly through observing ritual propriety (li 礼), and they will develop a sense of shame, and moreover, will order themselves", which emphasizes the guiding function of propriety towards law (Ames & Rosemont, 1998), that is, law should be established and construed in accordance with propriety. In Chinese legal system, "propriety" and "law" are two different but indivisible concepts. Both are evolved from social conventions and customs. Propriety functions as the standard of law while law facilitates the enforcement of law. What is allowed by propriety shall never be prohibited by law, and, in turn, what is forbidden in law will surely be against propriety. The relationship between propriety and law can be described as independent and interdependent at the same time, as they share the same origin but plays different roles in national governance. The combination of propriety and law is the most salient feature that distinguishes the Chinese legal system from other legal systems in the world, without which no true understanding of Chinese legal system may ever be reached (Zhu, 2013).

With respect to value of life, the Chinese legal system shows a strong inclination for humanism. "Benevolence" is the core concept of Confucianism, as well as the highest moral principle, moral standard and moral realm. "The benevolent loves others" advocated by Confucianists focuses on the discovery, respect and appreciation of human value. As stated in *Mengzi*, "Of the first importance are the people, next comes the food of land and grains, and of the least importance is the ruler" (Zhao &

Zhou, 1999). stressing the value of human being in the overall governance structure of a state and laying the theoretical foundation of ancient humanism in China. The Chinese legal system, being deeply influenced by such ideology, develops such legal principles as "put people first", "morality guiding and punishment supplementing", "integrate punishment with education" and otherwise.

2. Family-Oriented Law Being of Vital Importance in Overall Legal System

Throughout the history of ancient Chinese law, the family-oriented law has always been a fundamental part with indisputable importance. Karl Marx argued that each production mode would create its corresponding legal right relation and government form (Marx & Engels, 1995). Proverbially, Ancient Roman law is established on individualism and right orientation, ancient Chinese law, on the contrary, is established on collectivism and obligation orientation. Under the background that patrilineal family is the most fundamental social organization form, such collectivism has resulted in a strong family orientation in Chinese legal system. Xunzi once said, "In physical power humans are not as good as an ox, in swiftness they do not equal the horse; yet the ox and horse can be put to their use. Why is that? I say it is because humans alone can form societies and animals cannot" (Knoblock, 2003). In other words, the reason for humans being the only specie at the top of the food chain is that humans can unite as one and use the power of "group", which guarantees early humans' survival and development in severe natural environment. While in feudal society, the "group" equals to family. Family is the most basic unit in social production and living, as well as the smallest organization bearing the obligations of paying taxes, performing military service, implementing infrastructure construction and otherwise.

The characteristic of family orientation in the Chinese legal system is formed by natural selection rather than logical selection. In feudal times, the static and self-sufficient economy with poor productivity and underdeveloped agriculture decides that humans must form group in order to conduct production activities, therefore developing a labor organization form on basis of family. Multiple independent families unite as a clan, that is, a big family, through patrilineal consanguinity and, under the leadership of the patriarch, carry out a series of activities, such as obtainment of means of production, execution of production, creation of wealth, continuation of bloodline and otherwise. In a big family, the patriarch is supreme in his power, but shall also assume great responsibilities. He should manage the overall production activities, make rational allocation of resources, and coordinate both the internal relations among the family members and the external relations with other families. As an old saying goes, "nothing can be accomplished without norms and standards". In order to ensure the justice and equity of management and establish authority within the family, the patriarch must establish reasonable and effective rules for reward and punishment of the clan members. Such domestic rules exercised by the head of a feudal household with an aim to regulate the conducts of members thereunder are, to some extent, the earliest as well as the most common form of laws in ancient China. With innovation of production tools, the productive force further develops. In order to exploit more resources for production and ensure the security and prosperity of the family, big patrilineal families start to look for allies and the alliance so established is exactly the embryo of a feudal state. For example, many vassal states of China in the pre-Qin period are consisted of several big patrilineal patriarchal families. Since state is the unity of families, "law of the state" is nothing but extraction and integration of social conventions at the time and "rules of the family". To sum up, family rules lay the theoretical foundation for the state laws while the state laws enhance the validity of family rules.

Mencius said, "the world is based on the state, the state on the family, and the family on the individual" (Zhao et al., 1999). Family is the basic unit of the state, meaning that the internal order of family is of great significance for social stability and state governance. Rulers of previous dynasties have all stressed out that "family" and "state" are a community with shared future, recognizing the unshakable position of family in the integral state governance structure. As the patriarch helps the local government to fulfill certain responsibilities and functions like regulation of family members, payment of taxes, settlement of disputes, and implementation of policies and decrees, the state, in turn, acknowledges the absolute control of the patriarch over the family and endorse the patriarchal family system by law, legalizing the ethical relationship and hierarchy with the family. Taking the *Tang Code* as an example, in the "ten categories of major crimes", there are four categories of crimes directly involving family relationships, which are "*E'ni*" (premeditated assault and murder of elder kin), "*Buxiao*" (curse, sue or refuse to support one's grandparents and parents; conceal the death of grandparents and refuse to hold a funeral; held wedding ceremony and organize recreational activities during the funeral of elder kin), "*Bumu*" (assault, denounce or murder one's spouse, elders or relatives), and "*Neiluan*" (commit adultery with concubine of grandfather or father), vividly reflecting the family orientation of Chinese legal system (Zhangsun, 1983). Within such legal system, there is no firm boundaries between the ethical obligations for the family and legal obligations for the state, both family rules and state laws are adopted to maintain social order and enhance autocratic rule. The two kinds of laws, though having different theoretical basis, shares the same spirit and supplements each other in implementation. In a word, obvious family orientation is one of the unique features of Chinese legal system.

3. Emperor Holding Both Legislative and Judicial Powers

Legislative system and judicial system are two major branches in the framework of a legal system. It is thus necessary to analyze and summarize the features of these two systems in discussion about the characteristics of Chinese legal system. From 211 BC when Qinshihuang, the first emperor of China, established the first unified feudal state in the history to 1911 AD when the feudal and autocratic rule of Qing dynasty was overthrown by revolutionists under the leadership of Sun Yat-sen, China has been a feudal centralized country with emperor as its center of power for over two thousand years. Rulers of each and every dynasty would, after seizure of power, take various measures to consolidate his new-born regime, therefore continuously enhancing the autocracy in political institution. As stated in *The Book of Poetry*, "Everywhere beneath the sky, the king's immense lands do lie. Everywhere within the land, all obey the king's command" (Wang, 2008), the emperor rules all and the power structure centered thereon has the following features. Firstly, the emperor holds supremacy as the head of the state. His position of power sustains till he dies and will pass by inheritance to an heir generation by generation. The power of an emperor is perpetual from the time dimension and infinite from the spatial dimension; secondly, all organs of government are working bodies or agencies of the emperor, being responsible for nothing but execution of orders issued thereby. There is no entity that can truly balance or restrict the imperial power, let alone compete against the emperor to any extent; thirdly, the emperor is omnipotent as the perfect combination of divinity, sociality and humanity (Liu, 2000). In such a society, the emperor not only occupies all powers above the law, but also makes the whole country and all subjects his private properties.

On one hand, the emperor controls the paramount power of legislation. Since in Zhou dynasty, there is a dominant argument, "ritual propriety (*li* 礼), music (*yue* 乐), and punitive campaigns are initiated by the emperor" (Ames, 1998), indicating that the will of emperor is the primary source of law. The edict issued in the name of the emperor is a form of law with the supreme status, as well as the most authoritative doctrine guiding national activities and judicial practices. Where there is a conflict between the edict and the law, the former shall prevail. As the first feudal monarch in Chinese history, Qinshihuang seized the legislative power in his hands and even had special titles for his personally issued orders. The orders relating to major institution of the state are called "*zhi*(制)" while the orders relating to specific affairs are called "*zhao*(诏)". In Song Dynasty, Emperor Huizong once expressly announced that "With respect to the issuance of decree and enactment of law, the ultimate decision shall lie with the sovereign" (Xu, 2004a, 2004b, 2004c). In Ming Dynasty, the legislative power, in principle, remained to be the exclusive power of the emperor, who, as a result, is required to participate in the overall process regarding the formulation and promulgation of important laws and regulations. When the first draft of *Da Ming Lü* is completed, Zhu Yuanzhang, the founding emperor of Ming Dynasty, also released a special edit, requiring the officials participating in formulation of the Code to "report the detailed terms and conditions so formulated on a daily basis to let him decide in person" (Xu, 2004a, 2004b, 2004c).

Relevant examples are too numerous to mention. In a word, once the legislative power is controlled by the emperor instead of independent legislation authority, the nature of law has changed from a governance tool owned by the state to that owned by the emperor himself. The core values of law, which are fairness and justice, are ruined since the imperial power is above the law.

On the other hand, the emperor holds the absolute judicial power as the most powerful judge. First of all, the emperor owns the most comprehensive jurisdiction since all cases involving capital felonies, of significant social impact and with major disputes shall be judged and approved thereby. Taking the approval of the death penalty as an example, during the Wei Jin period, when it comes to determination of death penalty, no punishment may ever be executed without submitting to the emperor for approval in advance. If anyone is convicted and punished without approval, the law officer in charge will be punished. What's more, the emperor may, at will, impose punishment on anyone under his rule regardless of any law or statute. The old saying that "To be in the king's company is tantamount to living with a tiger" seems to be true. People could be deprived of their properties or even have the whole family be executed simply for saying something provoking discontent of the uppermost ruler. Examples of arbitrary punishment ordered by the emperor without judgement in accordance with laws abound in history. Last but not the least, the emperor also enjoys the power of absolution, which enables him to set free any offender violating the law. This power, to some extent, is like an ancient counterpart of the modern president pardon, but a limitless version. Originated in Han Dynasty, the "Danshu Tiequan" is a certificate of privilege granted by the emperor to his subjects making meritorious contributions to the state. The holder of such certificate can be spared from the death penalty for 1–3 times even when he or she has committed capital felony. For all intents and purposes, the law loses its independence and becomes a vassal of imperial power the very moment when the emperor seizes the judicial power.

4. An Uninterrupted and Purified Legal System Created by Multiple Nationalities

On one hand, the Chinese legal system is a legal system with strong national features. It is widely known that Chinese nation is a big family comprised of multiple nationalities in all ages. Though the Han nationality forms the major part, other nationalities also make irreplaceable contributions to the establishment and development of the Chinese nation. The Chinese legal system, thus, has integrated the legal consciousness and legal wisdom of different nationalities. As early as in ancient times, Miao people has created laws for punishment. According to *The Shu King*, "The people of Meaou were unmerciful in their regulations regarding punishments. They instituted five kinds of terrible inflictions and called them laws..." (Old, 1904), the five penalties so formulated were then adopted by the ruler of Huaxia people, namely, the Han nationality, and gradually developed into a prevailing system of punishment in Xia, Shang and Zhou Periods. The laws and regulations in Sui and Tang Dynasties could be regarded as the comprehensive expression of ancient Chinese legal system. However, the overall structure and the fundamental contents of laws in these two dynasties were designed and constructed by reference to the code implemented by the ruler of Xianbei nationality, which is, the *Law of the Northern Qi Dynasty*. Not only Han nationality would learn from legislation experiences of the minorities, the minorities, in turn, would also absorb the essence of legal system constructed by the Han nationality. In the later part of feudal society, almost each and every regime established by minorities like Xixia, Liao, Jin and Yuan, while preserving the essential features of their own nationalities, have formulated their laws and regulations on basis of laws and institutions of Tang and Song Dynasties. And the rulers of Qing Dynasty have even declared that all laws and regulations shall be formulated in accordance with the basic principle of "referring to the laws of Han nationality and considering the actual situations of Jurchen nationality". Thus, it could be concluded that the Chinese legal system is a unified combination of legal cultures and spirits of multiple nationalities. The incessant exchanges and mutual learning between different nationalities have endowed the Chinese legal system with ever-lasting vitality and rich diversity, making it stand towering in the world legal system community (Chen, 2005).

On the other hand, China is an independent state for thousands of years and its culture is one of the world earliest cultures. Created and developed by the Chinese nation, prospered and thrived in the mainland, the Chinese culture is an indigenous culture to the backbone. Though it has, in history, been rocked by foreign cultures for several times, the noumenon thereof has never been eroded. As an important branch of the Chinese culture, the traditional legal culture in China has treated the Confucianism as its one and only orthodoxy. "In Han and Tang Dynasties, Buddhist culture was introduced and spread in China. In Qing Dynasties, minorities even ruled the state. However, the legal system of China still remained unchanged. It had neither incorporated or mixed with doctrines of other legal systems, nor existed parasitically on any other legal system. The reason for such independence might be the purity of culture" (Zeng, 2009). Among all legal systems in the world, the Chinese legal system is the only legal system not mixing any foreign element or feature and all the institutions and ideologies thereof are invented and developed endogenously. It is widely held in the academic circle that "purity" is the essential feature that makes the Chinese legal system stand out as a major legal system. And such purity is formed due to a variety of underlying causes: as for the geographical conditions, China is an East Asian country with a large territory. The favorable geographic location and abundant natural resources created perfect conditions for long-term, stable development and autonomy; as for the economic type, ancient China was an agricultural country. With natural economy being the dominant type of economy, China developed an agriculture-oriented legal system regarding the protection and development of agriculture as its absolute and primary task and the closeness of agricultural production also resulted in the closeness and conservatism of legal system; as for the governance mode, autocracy has permeated into every aspect of social life, enhancing the closeness of culture and resulting in a lack of positive communication and exchange between the Chinese legal system and other legal systems; and as for the cultural elements, the Chinese culture stems from the Huaxia culture created by the Huaxia nationality. And the Huaxia nationality itself, in the first place, was an alliance of several different tribes and gradually developed into the strong, unified and dominant nationality in China over time. Such diversity in nationality composition has exerted propounding influences on legal culture, rendering it a culture incorporating multinational elements. Therefore, the Chinese legal system becomes a self-contained, purified legal system with inner openness and diversity (Chen, 2005).

3.4 The Influences of the Chinese Legal System

1. The Influences of the Chinese Legal System on East Asian Countries and Regions

The western culture had truly influenced and threatened the Chinese culture at the last reign of Qing dynasty when the great west powers intruded this ancient oriental empire. But before that, China has always been the leader among all East Asian countries and regions and the Chinese culture is also the one and only source for cultures developed in this area (Yang, 1999). Countries like Japan, Korea and Vietnam are all member states under the Chinese legal system. The legal institutions and systems of these countries, though distinguishing from each other with respect to the extent of imitation and scope of influence, have all inherited the core legal spirit and tradition created and developed by the Chinese nation. The East Asian legal culture formed on basis of Chinese legal system has flourished and developed into a powerful legal culture standing with the legal culture dominating the western world, that is, the Roman legal culture, as an equal.

As for state-to-state relations, there was a leader-member relationship between China and East Asian countries in ancient times since China used to be the suzerain state of its East Asian neighbors. Japan, Korea and Vietnam have all, in history, been the vassal states of China, yielding to the emperor of China, rendering tribute on a yearly basis, and accepting the titles conferred by the central government. A typical example thereof is Korea. As noted in the *History of Former Han Dynasty*, "After the end of Shang Dynasty, Jizi went to Korea, educated people thereof with rite and morality, brought about techniques of agriculture and textile, and established eight major prohibitive provisions" (Xu, 2004a, 2004b, 2004c). This statement indicates that Korea was the fief of Jizi in Zhou Dynasty and the eight provisions formulated by Jizi were the earliest statutes in the history of Korea. The superior-subordinate administrative relationship has resulted in Korea's transplant of Chinese legal system. As argued by Angus Hamilton, "The principles and character of Korean law presented no very marked deviation from that which had been upheld in China through so many centuries. The rigid and conservative legal system established and implemented by China has dominated Korea for so long…". Professor Yang Honglie also pointed out that all laws and regulations enacted by Korea before 1905 are imitation of Chinese laws (Yang, 1999). As for Vietnam, it used to be the southernmost part of China from Eastern Han Dynasty to late Tang Dynasty, during which the laws and regulations of China were promulgated and enforced as formal and official laws. After Five Dynasties and Ten Kingdoms Period, Vietnam declared its independence, but still recognizing China as its mother country. Thus, it can be concluded that, in ancient times, the leader-member relationship between China and other East Asian countries has laid a solid foundation for the top-down spreading of Chinese legal culture.

As for the degree of influences, the laws in East Asian countries are deeply influenced by traditional Chinese legal culture in all aspect since they are member states of the Chinese cultural circle. With regard to the historical origin of law, East Asian countries have all developed their own laws and regulations on basis of the Chinese law. Though distinguishing from each other in terms of traditions and customs, these countries do have one thing in common, that is, they all have one same parent law, the Chinese law. With regard to the manifestation form of law, statutory code is the most representative form of law in these countries. "Law" and "Order" constitutes the major part of such statutory code. With regard to the ideology of law, these countries, under the guidance of Confucianism, have formed an ideology integrating human sentiment, natural justice and legislation, which is radically different from that of other legal systems. With regard to the content and nature of law, these countries mainly focused on establishment and enactment of penal law and administrative law, written private law other than the family law were underdeveloped therein. With regard to the implementation of law, administrative organs and judicial organs at central government level assumed different functions and responsibilities while, below this level, the administrative organs took overall control of both administrative and judicial affairs. With regard to judicial adjudication, criminal cases were tried through rigid procedures and in strict accordance with laws while civil cases were mainly solved through settlement instead of judgement. With regard to the spirit and value orientation of law, laws in these countries were established to maintain the imperial rule and aimed at protecting social stability and interpersonal harmony. With regard to the knowledge type, legal science in these countries was more of a science focused on interpretation and annotation of law in accordance with feudal rites and imperial politics comparing to the western legal science (Zhang, 2007a, 2007b).

As for the method of influence, the Chinese legal system has exerted its influences on the East Asian countries mainly by official communication and learning activities led by the government. Among these countries, Japan is the one most affected by the Chinese legal culture and has achieved impressive accomplishments in introduction and transplantation of Chinese legal civilization. The Japanese law and legal framework are basically an imitation of that of China in ancient times. "Japanese law has belonged to the Family of Chinese law for more than one thousand six hundred years. Though dramatic changes have taken place after the Taika Reform, the moral philosophy and the ancestor worship custom and feudal system of China still function as the foundation of Japanese legal system", said Hozumi Nobushige in *Civil Code of Japan* (Zhang, 2007a, 2007b). The communication between China and Japan can be traced back to the first century AD when Liu Xiu, Guangwu Emperor of Eastern Han Dynasty, granted a golden seal to the envoys from Japan as a reward for all efforts they put in coming to China from afar. In 238 AD, Himiko, the legendary queen of Yamataikoku (a state established in the northeast part of the Kyushu Island), had sent envoys to China to seek an audience with the emperor of Wei state. From the beginning of the seventh century to the end of the ninth century, Japan had assigned its diplomatic mission to visit China for multiple times. The diplomats came from Japan, also called Kentoushi, stayed in China in order to get a full experience and thorough understanding of Chinese culture. They then brought back the advanced legislation and legal construction experience to Japan and facilitated the rulers to redesign their legal framework and reform the political institution therein. At this stage, the traditional legal culture of China has revolutionized the way in which Japanese ruling class govern the society and resulted in the famous Taika Reform in history. The official Sino-Japanese cultural exchanges tapered off when Japan entered into the Shogunate Period (1192–1867). During this period, Japan no longer applied the laws and legal institution of China indiscriminately like in Tang Dynasty. Instead, it utilized the Chinese laws and institutions as a template and established its own legal system with Japanese characteristics in accordance with basic national conditions thereof. But Chinese legal system still served as the primary source of study since there is no other legal system available for reference. For example, laws and regulations enacted in this period like *Temporary Criminal Law of Japan* are formulated by reference of laws and regulations in Ming Dynasty (Liu, 1996). Speaking of the successful transplantation and application of Chinese legal system, the contributions of official cultural exchanges initiated by government of both sides cannot go unnoticed. Such communication activities not only boosted the mutual understanding and cooperation between the two countries, but also enhanced the influences of Chinese legal system on outer world.

2. The Influences of the Chinese Legal System on the Western World

China has long established relationships with the western countries. During the Warring States Period, ethnic minority in the northwest already have sold the silk of China to the Middle Asian and the merchants thereof resold it to the Europe. In 138 BC, Liu Che, Emperor Wu of Western Han Dynasty, dispatched Zhang Qian on a mission, the initial purpose of which is to seek allies in the west with a view to jointly fighting against the northern tribes. However, Zhang Qian's travel to the west opened the famous Silk Road, which played an important role in facilitating communication and economic cultural exchanges between China and the west. The Silk Road, after centuries of expansion, reached as far as the ancient Rome. The Chinese merchants exported the silk, tea and porcelain to the countries and regions along the Silk Road, bringing along the traditions, customs and certain laws and regulations concerning business transactions of China as well (He, 2002).

It was in the Middle Ages when Chinese legal culture aroused obvious attention of the western world. In *The Travels of Marco Polo*, there are clear descriptions on Chinese family law and penalty system of Yuan Dynasty. After the sixteenth century, western scholars had carried out deeper studies on Chinese legal culture and proposed tremendous critics and profound insights regarding all aspects of Chinese legal system. G. W. Leibniz, the great German philosopher and jurist, have introduced laws of China in his *Novissima Sinica: Historiam Nostri Temporis Illustratura* published in 1679, in which he argued that "China is a great country with smaller territory but larger population and superior national governance than that of the civilized Europe" and recommended that Chinese legal culture and the western legal culture can complement and balance each other (Pang, 1991). F. M. Voltair, as a sincere advocate of Confucius and Confucianism, also had a very high regard for Chinese law at that time, "The two things that Chinese people make the greatest efforts to understand, cultivate and complete are morality and law". As he argued, "in other countries, laws are applied to punish crime. But in China, the function of law extends as it is also used to reward good deeds" (Voltair, 1995), the combination of morality, politics and law has endowed the Chinese legal system with eternal vitality.

As there are tremendous differences in geographical environment, traditions and customs, and economic and political institutions between the East and the West, the influences of Chinese legal system on the western world are limited mainly in the academic circle and the institution and legal practices therein are barely affected. The promotion of Chinese legal system therein exhibits three basic features as follows.

First of all, the promotion of Chinese legal system in western countries is mainly achieved by peaceful communication instead of by war or conquer. As stated in The Shu King, "An intelligent king being mindful of his principles, foreigners form all garters approach him with profound respect". Guided by the Confucian doctrine, the central government of each dynasty in the Chinese history basically followed the principle of "subdue men by virtue" when handling relations with other countries and tried to promote an international relation framework of "treating foreign nations with courtesy and guiding the people with kindness", under which the interactions among different countries shall be in conformity with rite and law. These two constitutes the general code of conduct universally observed by all Chinese and the standards implemented by the central government in dealing with international relations. And the promotion of Chinese legal culture is no exception.

What's more, foreign merchants, diplomats and missionaries were the main force in the promotion of traditional Chinese legal culture in the western world, among which the missionaries played a decisive role in this process and made the greatest contribution thereto. They are the well-deserved pioneers and founders for Sino-West legal cultural exchanges (Shi, 1999). From the fifteenth century, human society entered into the Age of Exploration. The discovery of new routes greatly shortened the distance between ancient China and the western countries. Whether the Jesuits came to China from Portugal, Italy and Spain in the middle of the sixteen century or the protestant missionaries from the Great Britain and America in the nineteenth century have all acted as an important intermediary in the cultural communication and promotion between the East and the West. Before coming to China, most of them have received systematic training for a relatively long period of time and accumulated abundant knowledge and skills. Many missionaries stayed in China for over 20 years and devoted themselves in the study and translation of Chinese classics, which enables them to form a comprehensive understanding of Chinese culture and traditions. During this process, the missionaries constantly introduced their experiences in and understanding of different aspects of Chinese society back to the West by reading notes, correspondences, writings, reports and otherwise, attracting extensive interests and attention in western society as well as laying the foundation for sinology research therein. In particular, the introduction and arguments related to Chinese law were perhaps the first-hand materials for the western academic circle to get to know Chinese legal culture. Taking the influences of Chinese legal culture on the Europe as an example, if we take a careful examination on the historical materials concerning Chinese legal culture cited by the European jurists, philosophers, ideologists and writers at the time, we will find that the classics so cited were all translated by the missionaries. Western scholars in the past barely visited China and their understanding and perception of China were generally formed by the descriptions and introduction made by missionaries, merchants and others who personally came and stayed in China and the Chinese classics so translated. Therefore, missionaries' travel in the ancient oriental empire is of great significance for the spreading of traditional Chinese legal culture in the western world.

Last but not the least, the outland promotion of traditional Chinese legal culture is relatively passive as it is realized mainly by conscious learning and arbitrary implementation of westerners in China. Whether in dynasties with high level of cultural openness like Han and Tang period or in dynasties when the central government adopted a foreign policy of seclusion like Ming and Qing period, very scarcely did the rulers in China actively promote their laws and culture to the outer world. Foreign countries and regions, no matter in or outside the Chinese cultural circle, have to be the active carrier of Chinese culture and complete the overall process of cultural transmission, that is, contact, selection and input, while China, the owner of its culture, stands by and only focuses on development and perfection of its own. There are three reasons for such passivity in transmission method. The first comes the cultural superiority. In ancient times, China was the incontestable super power in the East. It occupied the largest territory with most abundant resources ever since the Qin Dynasty and surpassed all other Asian countries and regions at the time with its strong economic power and extraordinary cultural deposits. The Chinese civilization, as it were, is not inferior in any aspect to any other civilization in the world. The Chinese people has always been proud of the long history and outstanding achievements of its culture and developed a cultural superiority in their national character. Therefore, when it comes to communication and exchange with foreign countries, the Chinese, driven by this mentality, are less willingly to learn from other cultures. Instead, they are more inclined to or opened to have others do the work. The second comes the cultural exclusivity. As mentioned above, the feudal autocracy with emperor holding the core powers in ancient China have deprived the independence of law and rendered it a pure tool for consolidation of the rule. The legal system and culture, together with other economic and political institutions and systems designed by the ruling class, jointly formed a complete and rigid national governance loop. Any factor coming from foreign civilization that may destabilize this loop will be immediately excluded or eliminated by the rulers without hesitation. The lase comes the limitations of objective cultural communication conditions. Though there did have exchanges between the East and the West in ancient times, the geographical distance and barriers and immature seamanship have determined that such communication can only be private, sporadic and in small scale. The cost for official, constant and large-scale cultural exchange is too expensive that neither China nor any western country in ancient times could afford.

3. Conclusion

Given the above, the promotion of traditional Chinese legal system in foreign world can be divided into two categories, one is the equal exchange among different legal systems and the other is the absorption and transplant of superior legal culture by the backward culture within the same legal system.

The former mainly refers to the interactive relationship between China and Europe in respect of legal culture exchanges. In the Age of Exploration, advances in science and technology made voyage around the world possible. Envoys, merchants and missionaries adventured to China from distant Europe, bringing in western culture. In the meanwhile, the philosophy, history and legal culture were also transmitted to Europe. The eighteenth century witnessed a "sinomania" spreading across the Continent. The philosophers, ideologists and artists were fascinated by the mysterious ancient oriental culture and considered it a precious repository for inspiration of new thoughts. They tried to find some arguments that can support their theories in the traditional Chinese legal culture and carried out analysis and review of Chinese legal thoughts, theories and system from the standpoint of a critic. Some of them thought highly of this foreign legal culture while others not. But no matter what kind of conclusion they have obtained in the end, the fundamental premise for drawing such a conclusion is that they have recognized and accepted that traditional Chinese legal culture is indeed a competent counterpart to that of their own. This lays the foundation for equal Sino-Europe cultural exchanges. Unlike the East Asian countries, European countries inherited the civilization of ancient Greece and Rome and had developed a relatively comprehensive legal culture. In regard to legal system, there were Roman Law, Germanic Law and Canon Law growing in the Continent, constituting an integrated legal system. Both the Chinese legal system and the European legal system are cultivated and matured in its unique political and cultural environment and both held the unquestionable leading position within their own turfs. Therefore, the influences of Chinese legal system on the Europe are bound to be equal communication and exchange. In addition, Europeans, like the Chinese favoring their legal culture, also possess strong confidence in and a sense of superiority towards the legal culture of the Continent, which having resulted in an inevitable preference and subconscious inclination in their understanding and comprehension of traditional Chinses legal system. Whether the result is objective or not, the comparative studies concerning Sino-west legal systems carried out by the westerners have confirmed the influences of Chinese legal system on the foreign world.

The latter appertains to the imitation and localization of legal thoughts, culture and institution by member states within the Chinese legal system. Before the rise of Western colonialism, there is an outstanding regional order in the Asia called "Chinese rule-of-rite system". With the feudal government of China being the center of authority and rule-of-rite as the guiding principle, this system has played a positive role in maintaining and stabilizing bilateral and multilateral relations between and among China and its neighboring countries and region (Huang, 1992). In this system, China is the one dominating the development of the whole area in all aspects. Politically, there is a suzerain-vassal relationship between China and the East Asian countries and regions. Economically, China is the biggest economy with abundant resource, strong productivity and well-developed economic system. Culturally, all basic elements constituting the "East Asian cultural circle" including Chinese character, Chinese-style law and decree system, agricultural and industrial techniques, Taoism and Sinicized Buddhism have imposed magnificent impact on the language, ideology, social structure, and productivity of countries and regions in East Asia. As an integral part of traditional culture, the Chinese legal system also lies at the heart of East Asian legal culture and has become the standard for member states' imitation and transplantation. Comparing with China, these countries during the same period lagged behind as they usually did not have independent and integrated legal institution and framework. So, in order to realize effective national governance, maintain social stability and promote rapid development, they all made the choice of transplanting and internalizing the Chinese laws and legal institution based on their special national situations to establish their own in a fast and effective manner. Such all-around imitation is the most prominent presentation for the influences of traditional Chinese legal system on the outer world, as well as a demonstration of the value and vitality thereof.

3.5 Significance of the Rejuvenation of Chinese Legal System

In the above-mentioned classification of world legal systems, the Chinese legal system has been widely recognized as an independent legal system with distinct features and far-reaching influences. This legal system can be dated back as early as in the first century BC. After a long period of modification and optimization, it matured in the eighth century and gradually developed into a China-centered legal system with the scope of influence covering the East Asia or even the overall Asia area. The First Opium War in June 1840 has brought seismic changes to Chinese society and nationhood and revolutionized the way in which Chinese people think of themselves and the world. The strong military power of the West forced China to open to the world after 300 years of seclusion while the accompanying modern legal culture also struck the traditional Chinese legal system a heavy blow, after which the self-enclosed Chinese legal culture under a longitudinal inheritance mode was made to communicate with the western legal culture horizontally. By the early twentieth century, the feudal society of China finally fell apart. The Chinese legal system, as a derivative of feudal system culture, lost its foundation of independent existence and became a "dead legal system" (Chen, 1980). Though the collectively created and time-tested Chinese legal system disintegrated due to a combination of internal social-economic structure change and external capitalist colonial invasion, the rich legal culture deposits thereof and well-developed social governance theory and practice had played a significant role in adjusting social relations and stabilizing social order. Nowadays, many people hold that the Chinese legal system has lost its original vitality and become obsolete as it failed to keep abreast of the time, but the in-depth impacts imposed by the legal consciousness and ideology derived from traditional legal culture on a nation's social structure can never be eliminated in the short run (Ge, 2009). The essence and ultimate value goal of Chinese legal system may be useful historical reference for facilitation of Chinese legal modernization, promotion of "the Belt and Road Initiatives", and contribution of Chinese legal wisdom to global rule-of-law construction.

The rejuvenation of Chinese legal system can facilitate the inheritance of the excellent traditional legal culture and identify the roots of modern Chinese legal system. It is widely accepted that globalization is an irresistible trend of the human society. With the deepening of economic globalization, legal globalization has also been considered an integral part of global development. Legal globalization, as the name implies, refers to the integration of legal systems and norms that adjust the same type of social relations. "During the process of global legal modernization, the legal life of China has gradually integrated into the global legal system" (Feng, 2002). Such concepts in the western legal culture as "human rights", "separation of powers", "democracy and freedom" and "inviolability of private property" has brought about a strong dash to the Chinese legal culture, but the impact is rather limited because it cannot or will not touch the inherent qualities thereof. The Chinese legal system is people oriented, values moral education, cares for the old and the young, imposes punishment cautiously, and prefers mediation in settling social disputes. These qualities are formed in the unique social, economic and legal environment of China and carry peculiar ideology, wisdom and connotation of traditional legal culture. "Even in the time of globalization when the world gradually integrates as a whole and the commonality in development of law tends to increase, the modernization of world legal system, to the contrary, shows a high degree of diversification instead of integration. The specificity in the development of law is exactly the significance of global legal modernization. The laws with national characteristics and local traits are, to all intents and purposes, laws with globality and internationality" (Gong, 2002). During the construction of a legally modernized country, prudent and reasonable absorption and utilization of the above-mentioned qualities would bring something inspiring to the modern Chinese legal system, enrich the Chinese legal culture, enhance the national cultural soft power, improve legal literacy of Chinese people and promote the modernization of national governance system and governance capacity.

The rejuvenation of Chinese legal system can upgrade the rule of law of China and boost the development of "the Belt and Road Initiatives". On one hand, the rule-of-law construction in China has accomplished remarkable achievements over the past 40 years of reform and opening-up. However, it cannot be denied that China, as the parent country of the Chinese legal system, still has a long way to go with respect to its rule-of-law construction comparing to England, the parent country of the common law system, and France, the parent country of the civil law system, that have developed and modified their rule-of-law design for hundreds of years. Therefore, the most fundamental goal of rejuvenating the Chinese legal system lies in promoting the rule-of-law construction of China, putting it on par with that of parent countries of other modern legal systems in the near future. According to the rule-of-law construction goals of China, "the rule of law for the country, the government, and society is basically in place. Institutions in all fields are further improved, the modernization of China's system and capacity for governance is basically achieved" by the 2035, and "the modernization of China's system and capacity for governance is achieved" by the 2050 (Xi, 2017). A relatively complete rule of law is conductive to the standardization of various acts and activities occurred in the implementation of "the Belt and Road Initiatives", settling disputes arising therefrom and securing the progresses of the Initiatives. On the other hand, the rejuvenation of Chinese legal system includes not only the promotion of rule-of-law of its parent country, but the construction and development of the member states. The parent country and the member states all belong to one legal system and thus can be referred to as a "modern rule-of-law community" (Wang, 2018). There should be certain commonalities between the rule of law in the parent country and that of the member states, which can provide the basis for positive communication and friendly negotiation among different members in case of disagreements and disputes. Currently, the rule of law in countries that have echoed the "the Belt and Road Initiatives" varies considerably and such unevenness has already brought about some side effects for the economic and trade cooperation, which means further steps need to be taken to close the gap. Therefore, in order to narrow the gap of rule of law among different countries under one legal system, guarantee the fair and even exchange, improve regional cohesion and increase efficiency in communication and cooperation thereof, we should strive to construct the member states of Chinese legal system in a new age and promote the establishment of a regional rule-of-law community composed of countries joining the "the Belt and Road Initiatives".

The rejuvenation of Chinese legal system can push the global rule-of-law construction with Chinese wisdom. The traditional Chinese legal system is a great contribution made by China to the world legal system construction. However, in the reformatory tide of global legal modernization, the traditional Chinese legal system gradually stepped down from the stage of history. Rejuvenation of Chinese legal system may not only revitalize this old and "dead" legal system and turn it into a new and modernized one, but also expand the family of global modern legal systems and alter the existing setup thereof. In today's world, there are only two modern legal systems—the common law system and the civil law system—that are of considerable practical significance, while "Indian legal system, Islamic legal system, and Chinese legal system headed into extinction silently" (Cheng, 1934). As we can see, the parent countries of the two living legal systems are western countries, which means no parent country for modern legal system in the east. By rejuvenation of the Chinese legal system, it may be possible to change the status quo and establish a new and independent modern legal system completely different from its western counterparts, therefore enhancing the diversity in form and organization of modern world legal systems. In addition, the contribution to world legal system construction is, in fact, a contribution to the global rule-of-law construction. The rule of law has now become a widely recognized and globally adopted strategy of national governance, but the rule of law in different countries and regions distinguishes from each other owing to their special national conditions. The modern legal system itself could be described as a centralized reflection of such uniqueness. Thus, the rejuvenation of Chinese legal system aims at constructing a rule of law different from rule of law in other countries, that is, a socialist rule of law with Chinese characteristics, and transforming China, the country representing one fifth of the total world's population, into a country under the rule of law.

References

Ames, R. T., & Rosemont, Jr., H. (1998). *The analects of Confucius*. Ballantine Books.
Chen, C. (1980). A study on characteristics of Chinese legal system. *Chinese Journal of Law, 1*, 48–53.
Chen, G. (2005). *Chinese culture and Chinese legal system—Collected works of legal history by Chen Guyuan*. China University of Political Science and Law Press.
Cheng, S. (1934). A study on Chinese legal system. *Law Review, 11*, 3–5.
Feng, Y. (2002). *Globalization and response of Chinese legal institution*. Sichuan People's Publishing House.
Ge, Z. (2009). On rejuvenation of Chinese legal system. *Legal System and Society, 23*, 3–5. https://doi.org/10.19387/j.cnki.1009-0592.2009.23.002
Gong, P. (2002). *Jurisprudence*. Fudan University Press.
He, Q. (2002). A study of Chinese legal culture's influences on foreign states before the Opium War. *Jianghai Academic Journal, 3*, 125–127.
Huang, Z. (1992). *A study of Chinese theoretical system I: China-led order in Asia—A discussion on form of relations between and Asian countries*. China Renmin University Press.
Huang, Z. (2012). Chinese law system and world legal systems—Academic history study from legal system to legal style. *Legal Science Magazine, 9*, 43–49. https://doi.org/10.16092/j.cnki.1001-618x.2012.09.009
Jeong, I. (2014). *History of Korea*. Southwest China Normal University Press.
Liu, J. (1996). *History of Sino-Japanese cultural exchange: Legal system*. Zhejiang People's Publishing House.
Liu, Z. (2000). Stratification study of social forms and discussion on ruler's dominance over society. *Historical Research, 2*, 12–14.
Marx, K., & Engels, F. (1995). *Collected works by Marx and Engels*. People's Publishing House.
Ma, X., & Shi, T. (2012). *Output and response: A study on foreign influences of traditional Chinese legal culture*. China Renmin University Press.
Old, W. G. (1904). *The Shu King: Or, the Chinese historical classic, being an authentic record of the religion, philosophy*. Theosophical Publishing Society.
Pang, J. (1991). *Image of China: Comments on Chinese culture by foreign celebrities*. Hubei People's Publishing House.
Qiao, W. (1986). On basic features of Chinese legal system. *Journal of Literature, History & Philosophy*, 2, 46-51.
Shi, T. (1999). *A study of Chinese legal culture's influences on the West*. Hebei People's Publishing House.
Voltair, F. M. (1995). *Essai Sur Les Moeurs* (Vol. I). Commercial Press.
Wang, L. (2018). Implementation of "the belt and road" initiative and rejuvenation of Chinese legal system. *Law and Modernization, 3*, 23–31.
Wang, R. (2008). *The book of poetry II*. Hunan People's Publishing House.
Wigmore, J. H. (1928). *A panorama of the world's legal systems*. Gaunt Inc.
Xi, J. (2014). *Decision of the CPC Central Committee on major issues pertaining to comprehensively promoting the rule of law*. Retrieved October 28, 2014, from http://www.gov.cn/zhengce/2014-10/28/content_2771946.htm
Xi, J. (2017). Xi Jinping's report at 19th CPC National Congress. *Xinhuanet*. Retrieved November 3, 2017, from http://www.xinhuanet.com/english/special/2017-11/03/c_136725942.htm
Xu, J. (2004a). *Full translation of twenty-four histories: The history of former Han Dynasty* (Vol. II). Chinese Dictionary Publishing House.
Xu, J. (2004b). *Full translation of twenty-four histories: History of Song Dynasty* (Vol. III). Chinese Dictionary Publishing House.
Xu, J. (2004c). *Full translation of twenty-four histories: History of Song Dynasty* (Vol. VII). Chinese Dictionary Publishing House.

Yang, H. (1999). *On influences of Chinese laws and regulations on East Asian countries*. China University of Political Science and Law Press.
Zhao, Z., & Zhou, D. (1999). *Mengzi*. Hunan People's Publishing House.
Zhang, J. (1984). Re-discussion on several issues of Chinese legal system. *Journal of CUPL, 2*, 6–16.
Zhang, J. (2007a). Fresh discussion of Chinese legal genealogy. *Journal of Nanjing University (Philosophy, Humanities and Social Science, 1*, 111–117+124.
Zhang, Z. (2007b). From Chinese legal genealogy to East Asian law—Legal tradition of East Asia and its change and trend. *Journal of Nanjing University (philosophy, Humanities and Social Sciences), 1*, 118–124.
Zhangsun, W. (1983). *The Tang code*. Zhonghua Book Company.
Zeng, X. (2009). *Study on legal culture* (Vol. 5). China Renmin University Press.
Zhu, J. (2013). Chinese law in the study of comparative law—Reflections on role of law in the society and the organizational form of powers. *Chinese Journal of Law, 4*, 80–98.

Chapter 4
Chinese Legal Classics and Translation

4.1 Introduction

The strategy of Chinese culture "Going Global", a national strategy concerning cultural construction put forwarded on early twenty-first century, has been steadily implemented for nearly 20 years, scoring such substantial results and tremendous achievements. For example, the "Library of Chinese Classics", the very first national major publishing project initiated by the National News Publication Bureau aiming at providing and promoting foreign versions of traditional Chinese cultural classics to the world in a systematic and comprehensive manner, has already delivered the foreign version or versions of over 110 Chinese cultural classics ranging from multiple fields and disciplines such as literature, history, philosophy, economy, military science, technology and otherwise (Wang, 2019). With joint efforts of the government, scholars and foreign sinologists, those translated versions have been fully accredited by the public, facilitating the spreading of Chinese culture. Since Chinese legal classics contains abundant traditional Chinese legal thoughts, wisdom and theories that are of great significance in improving the rejuvenation of Chinese legal system and directing our practices in comprehensively promoting the rule of law, the foreign promotion of these classics undoubtedly becomes a pivotal task in the implementation of Chinese culture "Going Global". However, on international level, it should be acknowledged that there is still obvious "deficit" between the outward communication of Chinese legal classics and the inward infiltration of western legal culture; while on domestic level, little research has been done with respect to the systematic and comprehensive introduction and promotion of legal classics comparing with other cultural classics and the foreign translation and review work thereof still faces certain difficulties and challenges both theoretically and practically.

The traditional Chinese legal classics carry and contain the legal wisdom of Chinese nation accumulated in the evolvement of Chinese legal system for thousands of years. The translation and promotion thereof will not only enhance our cultural soft power, but also contribute Chinese wisdom to global governance (Dong, 2018).

X. Dong and Y. Zhang, *Chinese Legal Translation and Language Planning in the New Era*, https://doi.org/10.1007/978-981-19-8448-8_4

This thesis analyzes the significance of translation of Chinese legal classics from the perspectives of rejuvenation of Chinese legal system and promotion of Chinese culture "Going Global", discusses the current research status and the problems and challenges encountered, and verifies the feasibility pertaining to the promotion and acceptance of Chinese legal classics in foreign cultures, with a view to presenting excellent Chinese legal culture to the world, rejuvenating Chinese legal system, enhancing China's discourse power concerning rule of law, and contributing Chinese legal wisdom to global governance.

4.2 Classics and Its Legal Cultural Significances

1. Definition of Legal Classics

"Classics is a kind of special social products reflecting certain thoughts and consciousness of human beings, including human science, social science, science and technology and otherwise" (Liu, 1998). Our ancestors have accumulated rich experiences and lessons during national governance practice of thousands of years and produced an immense number of legal classics. As we can see, there is a duality in the internal structure of legal culture, "one is the institutional legal culture, such as laws and regulations, legal system and otherwise; another is the conceptual legal culture, such as legal theories, legal psychology, legal customs" (Liang, 1992). Therefore, legal classics, as the carrier of legal culture, will inevitably be composed of substantial system and codes and ideal legal thoughts and theories.

In a broad sense, traditional Chinese legal classics not only involve laws, legislation, legal institution, but also cover ideology, culture and sociology. Thus, legal classics shall contain "written materials generated in legislation, judicial acts, law popularization, law interpretation, academic activities and otherwise, including official statutes, laws, regulations, decrees, orders, administrative and judicial instruments, judgement documents, legal science literature, practice reference, village rules, service guidelines, and otherwise" (Xu, 2019), as well as materials and contents relating to law in all cultural and art classics. According to the statistics of *General Catalogue of Ancient Books of China*, there are over 200,000 ancient books in China, among which "Books of Penal Code" alone accounts for nearly 800 therein. The *An Annotated Bibliography of Chinese Legal History* edited by Zhang Weiren has categorized legal literatures by norm, system, theory, and practice and recorded 2352 books and literatures, which is the most detailed and complete summary of legal literatures. As for the cultural an art classic involving law and legal affairs, the actual figure is too difficult and innumerous to be counted.

In a narrow sense, legal classics refer to the ancient codes and laws enacted or confirmed by the state with the enforcement of which being guaranteed by the coercive power of the state, including official code and its different supplementary forms. In accordance with incomplete bibliographic statistics, there are 160 official codes in China if we take the *Nine Chapters of Law* as the first and the *Ta Tsing Leu Lee* as the last (Hou et al., 1997). In addition to official codes, there are multiple supplementary legal forms such as "lv", "ling", "ge", "shi" and "chi". "lv" refers to the "laws that are considerably representative and relatively stable". It is the major form of ancient law but not the only form, which means the function and effect thereof are often supplemented and restricted by other legal forms. For example, there are "ling", "ke" and "bi" in Han Dynasty; "ge" and "shi" in Sui and Tang Dynasties; "chi" in Song Dynasty; "li" in Ming and Qing Dynasties. These supplementary legal forms are generally established in consideration of special national conditions and historical background and therefore possess stronger flexibility comparing to the official codes. However, many legal forms were lost or survived in fragments due to historical reasons, we may only have a restricted view thereon in the existing historical materials.

Additionally, ancient China is a unitary multi-national country with Han nationality being the principal part. Though the Han nationality has played a major role in the establishment of Chinese legal system, many minority ethnic groups have also made nonnegligible contribution thereto and achieved outstanding achievements in ethnic legislation, for instance, the *Mongolia Law*, *General Principles of Tibet*, *Regulations of Unger Xinjiang*, and otherwise formulated in Qing Dynasty are all integral legal wisdom contributed by minority ethnic groups to the Chinese legal system. In short, these precious ancient Chinese legal classics recorded the struggles and successes of legal practitioners, inherited and passed on the Chinese spirit of law, and moulded the legal cultural memory of Chinese nation as well as the overall East Asia region.

2. The Legal Cultural Significance of Legal Classics

Generally speaking, culture is a man-made environment developed by human beings through countless practices in order to survive. Therefore, from a cultural perspective, "legal culture, as a constituent part of human culture, integrates all activities in relation to law, legal thoughts, legal systems, legal enforcement in the social superstructure and the results thereof. It is the product of human legal activities as well as the manifestation for status and completion degree of real legal practices" (Wu, 1994). From a spiritual perspective, "legal culture can be construed as the spiritual part of legal phenomenon, that is, the integration of collective cognition, evaluation, mental state and behavior pattern concerning law and legal life accumulated during the process of social progress, which depends on the social economic basis and political structure" (Zhang, 1992). Like culture, legal culture is also characterized by nationality, regionality and diversity, resulting in the commonality in the way people from a specific national construe legal phenomenon, establish legal institutions and regulations, and engage in relevant legal practices. Legal classics are those classical texts in a nation's history written by intellectual elites specialized in law, politics and social governance, containing major legal wisdom of that nation and at the same time constituting the visible part of the legal culture. In such classics, records of institutions and regulations, descriptions of legal events, and assessment of legal phenomenon can be found. We may catch a glimpse of the overall legal system of such nation from those legal classics and they, undoubtedly, are of great legal cultural significances.

Firstly, "classics are major books and literatures written in characters passed down from history" (Zhao, 2014). Ancient Chinese, in accordance with their own practical activities, have summarized experiences and created countless cultural works. These works, on one hand, show Chinese nation's wisdom and spirit concerning transformation of external environment and, on the other hand, react on people's real practices by the values and concepts contained therein. Traditional Chinese classics, in some sense, can be deemed as a comprehensive conclusion of practical experiences and public values and a concentrated reflection of how generations of Chinese people gradually develop their knowledge classification, value judgement and survival skills during their understanding, contact and transformation of outer world (Zhang, 2013). They are the precious spiritual legacies left by the ancestors. Additionally, the cultural creation of classics is never a one-time effort as the classics possess strong cultural adaptability and can be deconstructed, interpreted and processed over and over again. Therefore, learning from classics and exploring the culture connotation contained therein will not only facilitate personal growth, but also benefit the sustainable development of Chinese nation.

Secondly, the classics function a carrier of legal culture. The values and ideology so contained and promoted constitute the core of Chinese legal culture and have played such cultural roles as establishing legal infrastructure, guiding public behavior, evaluating legal phenomenon, and facilitating development of rule of law. For example, the "rule-of-rite" system strongly advocated in Confucian classics suggests that an excellent rule shall use moral education as the dominant method and the punishment as the supplementary method. The legislation in all dynasties of China are subject to such ideology of "morality given priority over punishment", which led to a special legal framework of "lü" and "ling". In this framework, "lü" is functioning as the negative and ex post punishment tool that protects the target behavior pattern by exerting different levels of deterrence on the guilty ones during the execution of punishment while "ling" sets up the positive standards for people's behaviors and promotes such by means of moral education. All in all, it is the traditional legal ideology in the classics that influences the design and application of such special "lü-ling" system and supports the evolvement thereof.

Thirdly, classics also plays an important role in the transition of legal culture. The transition always takes place in an outside-in manner, which means the outer legal infrastructures, legal texts, organization and system changes from time to time while the inner core legal cultural ideology remains relatively stable. Hence, as the expression media of core legal cultural ideology, classics used to and will continue to perform such legal cultural function in order to realize smooth transition of value system and man-made environment. For example, in late Qing dynasty, the Chinese society had undergone radical changes. The old legal forms were abandoned to the ground and the implantation of western discourse had led to creation of plentiful western-style laws and regulations. However, the expression form of law may have changed a lot, people's apprehension and values shaped by the legal culture contained in those classics can hardly ever be in sync with the change of times. In the application of new laws at that time, since people were still deeply influenced by traditional legal values in the classics, such values were then mixed in the new laws to improve the public acceptability. Thus, the legal cultural change and reconstruction of China at that time shows a distinct feature of "westernized Chinese style".

In conclusion, as culture is a spiritual living environment created by human beings for the long survival of the species, the classics formed during the historical development can be called the paramount manifestation of a culture. It is the crystallization of wisdom showing a certain nation's understanding and transformation of natural environment and covers all institutional design, organization and agency settlement, legislation standard, enforcement pattern and application methods in relation to law. The evolvement and transition of legal culture take place when the ethical values and instructional rules expressed by legal classics act on legal system. However, the legal implantation and cultural transition of China in modern times reflect a one-sided tendency of negating the traditional. Under the mass legislation, there is a crisis of value fragmentation caused by excessive disavowal of traditional culture. And people, due to absence of united values, will not voluntarily respect and obey the specific laws and regulations in their daily life. Therefore, the demands for reconstruction of united legal values and elimination of the unsuitability of "westernized" laws and regulations have made the rejuvenation of Chinese legal system and reinterpretation and promotion of traditional Chinese legal classics imperative.

4.3 Research Status of Chinese Legal Classics Translation

The history of communication among different civilizations is actually a history of translation since it is neither appropriate nor possible to carry out cultural exchange without translation. To survey comprehensively on the foreign translation of Chinese legal classics, the interest of western world in Chinese legal system and rule-of-law culture can be traced back to more than 500 years ago. In sixteenth and seventeenth century, European merchants and missionaries travelled to China, wrote down their experiences and feelings about different aspects of China and brought such travel notes, which contains description and evaluation of Chinese legal culture, back to Europe. The Sino-foreign cultural exchange from thereon to mid-eighteenth century undergone twists and turns and developed in a relatively small scale and slow speed. After eighteenth century, foreign translation of Chinese legal classics finally ushered in a spring owing to the vigorous Sino-foreign cultural exchange. The legal translation since modern times have been focused on four major legal classics, which are *Ta Tsing Leu Lee*, *Xi Yuan Ji Lu*, *Tang Lü Shu Yi*, and *Da Ming Lü*. The foreign translation of Chinese legal classics can be classified into the three types in accordance with the purposes of translation, degree of completion and identity of translator.

1. Preliminary Understanding of Chinese Legal Classics

In the first place, the western missionaries and merchants learned about Chinese language and culture and studied classics for the purposes of carrying out transactions and preaching their religion belief in China, they tried to find the origins of Chinese culture, or in other words, the preferences of Chinese people, in the classics, in order to better realize purposes mentioned above. After years of living in China, they got to know Chinese language and culture well. They introduced what they saw and experienced in China either by travel notes or oral description to their compatriots, removing some of the mystery of this ancient oriental empire and further deepening westerners' understanding of China.

Marco Polo, the world-famous Italian explorer, travelled through Persia to China in 1275 and lived therein for 17 years. In his travelogue, *The Travels of Marko Polo*, he described China as a rich and advanced nation where the judges fulfill their duties with loyalty and selflessness and transactions are implemented in perfect order. Later, Juan Gonsales de Mendoza, a Spanish monk, compiled a book titled *Historia del Gran Reino de la China* in 1585 based on diplomatic reports, documents, correspondences and writings by order of the Pope Gregory XIII, giving a relative comprehensive description of legal culture of ancient China. The book "touches the essence of life in ancient China. Its publication marked the beginning of an era when a set of standards applicable for knowledge of China and its institutions can be utilized by the European academia" (Hudson, 1995). The book has promoted the political systems and laws of China to the Europe, attracting intense interest of Europeans on China, but unfortunately, it fails to directly refer to the original text of Chinese legal classics, rendering the contents concerning law nothing but subjective hearsay and reducing the authenticity to a great extent (Hu & Dong, 2018a, 2018b). During the latter half of the sixteenth century, Matteo Ricci, an Italian Catholic missionary who preached in China for 28 years, praised ancient China for multiple aspects of its political and legal culture (Gong, 2004).

By the end of eighteenth century, trade bustled between western countries and China, more and more foreigners came to China. In the coastal regions of that time, foreign sailors and merchants often conflicted with local people and criminal crimes involving foreigners took place occasionally, promoting them to pay attention to the most important code of China, namely, the *Ta Tsing Leu Lee*, and other relevant provisions governing criminal cases. After the Opium War, westerners started to build factories and churches in China, resulting in relevant civil disputes. In order to achieve efficient settlement, westerners then shifted their attention to the terms and provisions concerning civil disputes in the *Ta Tsing Leu Lee*. However, foreign society at that time still judged Chinese law under constant suspicion and criticism, or even institutional superiority and prejudice. Essentially, their translation of the *Ta Tsing Leu Lee* served for nothing but profiting by invasion and preaching.

2. Abridged Translation of Chinese Legal Classics

After getting the whole picture of Chinese legal culture and system, the westerners started to translate certain legal works to deepen their understanding of Chinese legal life and better facilitate their actions in China. During this process, a group of people who had great enthusiasm in China stood out. They were later given a name—sinologists. A sinologist refers to "a western scholar engaging in humanistic and social sciences researches of ancient and modern China", typical example of which is Matteo Ricci, one of the earliest pioneers and popularizers who had great interest in China and came and stayed herein for long period of time. These sinologists selected and translated certain chapters and sections of contents concerning Chinese legal system and delivered a description of China's social status to the western world (Liu, 2015). At this stage, selected works and abridged translation have dominated the translation and promotion of ancient Chinese legal classics.

There are two reasons for such dominance of selected and abridged translation. On one hand, the main purpose that motivates theses sinologists to translate legal classics is to assimilate Chinese culture. As the Industrial Revolution dramatically improved the social productivity, the rapidly expanded national power, the far more advanced technologies, as well as the fact that China at that time was rich but backward have altogether give rise to the superiority complex with respect to institution and culture within the western world. Such western cultural centralism is so strong and deep-rooted that these sinologists only chose to translate the parts that they are interested in and can help achieve their goals. As we can see from a handful of relevant review reports, the editors were eager to publish such abridged translation or introductory articles with personal preferences, showing their disapproval, expressly or impliedly, for the large quantity of capital cases, frequent execution of punishment and cruelty of public execution.

On the other hand, the Chinese legal classics generally have such characteristics as great length, complex structure, extensive contents, and high degree of specialization. And, most importantly, they are written in classical Chinese, which means the translator has to do both the intralingual translation to convert classical Chinese into vernacular Chinese and the interlingual translation to convert Chinese into other languages, enhancing the difficulty of translation as it takes much more time and energy to complete such dual translation efficiently. This explains why there are so little translation of Chinese legal classics. In the preface of *Ta Tsing Leu Lee*, Sir George Thomas Staunton bluntly described the language as obscure and the structure as intricate (Staunton, 2015). In a word, it is the subjective cultural superiority in combination with the objective linguistic difficulty that resulted in incomplete translation and poor promotion of Chinese legal classics in the foreign soil. Though foreign readers are bound to have prejudice against the legal institution, wisdom and culture presented by Chinese legal classics due to all sorts of differences between China and the west, the fragmented, misunderstood or even biased translation by the sinologists can hardly absolve itself from the blame.

3. Complete Translation of Chinese Legal Classics

The translation of Chinese legal classics has finally entered into a new stage of complete translation since nineteenth century, more specifically, the latter half of the nineteenth century. At this stage, not only sinologists had punished complete translation and research papers, the domestic scholars also joined in, with a view to giving a relatively authentic and comprehensive view of China and promoting Chinese legal culture in the western world. Though they have put great effort and energy therein and indeed obtained certain achievements, there is still a long way to go as so far only four Chinese legal classics had been translated into English and other languages in a complete manner.

As for the first Chinese legal classic being translated in a full version, the *Ta Tsing Leu Lee* is the last feudal code promulgated by the government of Qing Dynasty and represents the summit of traditional Chinese legal culture. In 1810, the complete English version translated by Sir George Thomas Staunton is published in London, marking the advent of full-translation stage. This translation has aroused great repercussion within the academic community. Later, Paul-Louis-Felix Philastre and P. Gui Boulais had delivered their French translation respectively in 1876 and 1924 (Su, 2003). In 1994, the Oxford University Press published another English version translated by William C. Jones, which is titled *The Great Qing Code* (Qu & Wan, 2019).

The *Xi Yuan Ji Lu* is a systematic medical jurisprudence monograph written by Song Ci in 1247, which is over 350 years earlier than the first forensic literature, the *DeRclationluc Medicorum*, in western history. In 1779, certain chapters of this book were translated and introduced by French translator and published in Paris; in 1862, De Grys translated the full text in Dutch and the forensic scientists there has attached great importance thereto; in 1873, Herbert A Giles, the well-known English sinologist, delivered his translation—*The His Yuan Lu*, or *Instructions to Coroners*, and published in installments in *The China Review or Notes and Queries on the Far East*; then in 1981, over a century later, Brain E McKnight, professor of the University of Hawaii specialized in history of China, punished another English translation titled *The Washing Away of Wrongs: Forensic Medicine in Thirteen-century China* (Chen, 2016). The book has made groundbreaking contribution to the development of modern forensic science since it witnessed the birth of a new discipline with independent theoretical system and techniques—the forensic science. It has been introduced to many countries and regions such as Netherlands, France, the UK, America, Japan and translated into 19 languages in total ever since its inception.

As for the *Tang Lü Shu Yi* and *Da Ming Lü*, the full translation of the former one is made by Wallace Johnson. The Princeton University Press had published his translation, *The T'ang Code*, in two volumes respectively in 1979 and 1997, which jointly constitute the only complete translation in foreign language of the *Tang Lü Shu Yi*. On the other hand, the translation of *Da Ming Lü* came out as the latest one. The University of Washington Press published the full English version translated by Jiang Yonglin, *The Great Ming Code*, in 2005 (Wang, 2018). This translation aimed at presenting the basic characters of the Code and promoting cross-cultural interactions between the East and the West.

Overall, the western academia's concern for Chinese legal classics had gone through hundreds of years. Different sinologists and scholars at home and aboard, though with different purposes, had exerted their utmost effort to study, translate and promote great legal works of ancient China in the western world and published four representative works in total, facilitating foreign readers, scholars and sinologists in capturing a panorama of the Chinese legal system and providing important first-hand materials for researchers interested in traditional Chinese legal institution. However, neither the quality nor the amount of complete translation can meet the current demands of academic research and cultural dissemination and there are certain problems and obstacles to be solved in order to improve the current situation.

4.4 Problems to Be Solved in Chinese Legal Classics Translation

Speaking of research on translation of Chinese legal classics, the result so far, no matter in terms of quality or quantity, leaves much to be desired. As for research at abroad, the achievements are limited to full translation of the four legal classics mentioned above and academic papers written by the translators or sinologists, for instance, the doctorial dissertation written by Wallace Johnson, the translator of the *Tang Lü Shu Yi*, based on the first three chapters of his translation (Johnson & Li, 1984) and 12 papers written by American scholars specialized in study of Chinese legal history, which used to be published on English journals and now included in the *Recent American Academic Writings on Traditional Chinese Law* published on 2004 (Karen et al., 2004). As for research at home, upon consulting relevant keywords on the CNKI net, there are approximately 40 articles and papers relating to translation of traditional Chinese legal classics published on academic journals and newspapers within the recent 30 years. The researchers coming from different areas of expertise generally carried out discussion and analysis on Chinese legal classics and the translation thereof from the research perspectives of and by the research paradigms of their own discipline. Scholars specialized in linguistics and translation studies basically focused on comparison and review of different translation and exploration of available translation methods and strategies; jurists and legal practitioners laid emphasis on comparison of Chinese and western legal culture; and historians preferred to analyze the history of translation and communication between the east and the west, as well as the influences thereof. In a word, there still lacks adequate attention and resources for study on translation of traditional Chinese legal classics.

As modern history shows, the translation of Chinese legal classics opened a window for the outer world to know Chinese legal culture and explore the spirit and connotation of Chinese legal system, promoting and enhancing the communication and mutual learning between the eastern and western legal cultures. The rise of translation of legal classics would definitely bring about the rise of translation studies and translation criticism. The diversity of research depends on the quantity and category of translation of legal classics. However, as mentioned above, there is an obvious asymmetry, both in quantity and category, between the Chinese legal classics and its translation, resulting in several problems to be settled.

Frist of all, the toughest problem that we are facing is that the existing translation of Chinese legal classics is too scarce to meet the demand of research, which is also the major cause for the overwhelming concentration of studies on the aforesaid four codes. There is no need to repeat the abundance of legal classics, but the translation available for research remains scant. The translation of official codes is an arduous task, let alone the translation of countless works relating to legal ideology and culture. In 1995, China launched the Library of Chinese Classics Project, which is the first national publishing project systematically and comprehensively promoting foreign language editions of traditional Chinese cultural classics to the rest of the world. So far, the Project has published over 110 ancient Chinese classics. However, among all these works, there is no true legal classics, not even one (Xiong, 2019). On that account, it's not surprising that foreigners know little or nothing about legal traditions and wisdom of China. Therefore, some scholars have advocated that, in the process of translation, the Four Books and Five Classics, as well as other literature, may not fully represent the "Chinese culture classics", such classics of law, medical science, historical science, ethnic culture and traditional skill shall also be included (Zhao, 2012).

What's more, research in a single discipline accounted for the vast majority of current researches on translation of Chinese legal classics and cross-disciplinary and systematic study has not even started. On one hand, more than half of the domestic research articles and papers relating to translation of legal classics placed emphasis on conversion on the textual level and discussed the translation by words, sentences and discourses. Failing to transcend the usual limitations of the original text, these papers usually downplay the communicating effect, cultural influence and historical significance of translation of legal classics. To actively respond to the strategy of Chinese culture "Going Global" and facilitate the rejuvenation of Chinese legal system, comprehensive research from such perspectives as mutual learning among civilizations and spreading of legal culture must be made with respect to translation of traditional legal classics, by which the new cultural connotation and communication value of the old legal classics can be truly appreciated and presented to the world. On the other hand, due attention has not been given to many potential translations of legal classics delivered by foreign sinologists as it should be owing to all sorts of reasons. For instance, in the 1970s, western missionaries have founded a series of English journals in China and introduced and translated several Chinese legal classics thereon. "George Jamieson and J. W. Jamieson have respectively translated certain provisions of the *Ta Tsing Leu Lee*; Herbert A. Giles have translated the first two volumes of the *Xi Yuan Ji Lu*; and George Jamieson also translated 9 cases of the *Xing An Hui Lan (Cases in Chinese Criminal Law)* and published in *The China Review*" (Li, 2017). These dust-laden historical materials are all precious resources for study of translation relating to Chinese legal classics. Their significance, in the new era, should be reviewed, redefined, reinterpreted and renewed.

Last but not the least, there lacks mature and effective mechanism for cultivation of professional translators of legal classics. The translation of traditional legal classics involves both intralingual translation and interlingual translation. The translators should not only possess extensive knowledge in the field of law and foreign language, but also master the comprehension, interpretation and translation of ancient Chinese texts. Hence, the translation of legal classics "puts forward a high demand of accuracy and legal translators, to some extent, are social elites" (Dong, 2016).

To deliver a successful translation, one should at first find a qualified translator or a competent translation team. However, we are still facing such problems as lack of scientific guidance in teaching practices, improper arrangement of teaching content and curriculum provision, students' lack of professional legal knowledge and legal culture literacy, deficiency in competent faculty, outdated teaching methods and otherwise in the process of cultivating professional talents for translation of legal classics (Zhang & Ye, 2010). Additionally, the translation of legal classics and cultivation of professional translators is still in the start-up stage. In China, few colleges and universities have offered legal translation courses and even fewer of them have established relevant major and discipline of legal translation. Taking Jiangsu province as an example, there are 134 colleges and universities in total. Only comprehensive universities like Nanjing University, Southeast University, Nanjing Normal University and Suzhou University have developed translation major and, among these universities, just Nanjing Normal University offered courses of legal translation (Li & Dong, 2015). What make things worse is that almost all of the legal translation courses currently offered are about translation of modern legal texts and none of them focuses on translation of ancient legal classics. The high requirements for skill, long time consumption and poor research output of translation of legal classics have kept many translators and scholars away. To break this deadlock, efficient and effective mechanism shall be established to cultivate professional translation talents for translation of ancient Chinese legal classics.

4.5 Translation of Chinese Legal Classics

1. Practical Needs for Translation of Chinese Legal Classics

(1) The Need to Rejuvenate the Parent Country of Traditional Chinese Legal System

In the late Qing dynasty, Shen Jiaben, one of the most outstanding jurists in China's modern history, carried out all-around amendment of the *Ta Tsing Leu Lee* and created a series of new statutes and codes after being designated as the Minister of Law Reform, opening the new chapter of legal modernization. During this period, the introduction of western law based on translation of legal literature forms an essential part of China's legal construction. In the nineteenth and twentieth century, there is neither much Chinese legal literature available for output translation, nor any competent legal translator. At this stage, China was in a lack of both awareness of and capital for output translation of legal classics while western countries, motivated by commercial profits and political interests, grabbed the initiative in interpretation of Chinese legal culture and translation of legal works. Thus, the traditional legal images so created are disconnected from the actual legal practices and needed to be rectified and endowed with new meaning.

With the new century coming, China has established relatively complete legal system and framework and cultivated batches of excellent legal talents. The importance of legal classics is gradually acknowledged and addressed. In the 19th National

Congress of the CPC, a great political judgement announcing "socialism with Chinese characteristics has entered a new era" had been proposed, pointing out the new historical development direction for China's modernization of rule-of-law with Chinese characteristics and rejuvenation of traditional Chinese legal system (Qu, 2012). The transition in concepts of legal construction reflects the grand picture of establishing the traditional legal cultural discourse system. Since the previous discourse system is not sufficient to provide solid theoretical foundation and ample interpretation room for both ancient and modern Chinese legal practices. It's time for the domestic scholars to carefully explore Chinese legal culture in the ancient legal classics, develop strong belief in our splendid culture, rethink the long-living legal traditions, extract representative legal concepts, establish the unparalleled legal discourse system and promote valuable traditional Chinese legal culture to the world, with the ultimate goal of rejuvenating China, the parent country of traditional Chinese legal system. In this process, translation of legal classics may be the most effective and convenient method.

(2) The Need to Seek Roots for the Modernization of Rule-of-Law with Chinese Characteristics

As stated in *Laozi,* "the tree big as a man's embrace began as a tiny sprout, the tower nine storeys high began with a heap of earth, the journey of a thousand leagues began with what was under the feet" (Waley, 1999). Though we have learned and "borrowed" many factors from the western legal culture and institution when establishing our modern legal framework, the inner spirit and principles are deeply rooted in our local born and bred Chinese legal culture. Now, to complete the modernization of rule-of-law with Chinese characteristics, we must turn to our past and find answers and solutions in the history. Only when we know what the real Chinese culture is, will we know how strong we can be; only when others know what the real Chinese culture is, will we be able to communicate fairly and effectively. The translation of traditional legal classics offers a valuable opportunity for current scholars to reconnect with our own legal culture, have a conversation with the past, and obtain an impartial evaluation towards the current modernization of rule-of-law with Chinese characteristics. Besides, the research on output translation of Chinese legal classics and summarization of relevant practices and experiences may also contribute to the formation of holistic Chinese experience and lay foundation for the construction of "Chinese discourse". Only when the China established its own discourse system and take the initiative in promoting its own legal culture, will the modernization of rule-of-law with Chinese characteristics be recognized and accepted universally.

(3) The Need to Improve Diversity of the World Legal Culture

The Chinese legal classics represent the essence of Chinese people's beliefs, thoughts, theories and practices about law and form an integral part of human civilization. Not only showing the unique ethnic features of Chinese nation, but the Chinese legal classics also contain multiple common values shared by human species, starkly confirming the famous saying, "the more ethnic-oriented, the more universally accepted". The communication between different legal cultures requires the translation of legal classics in different languages. With the improvement of the comprehensive national power, Chinese culture "Going Global" has become a common demand of our times and output translation of legal classics shoulders this critical mission of Chinese culture "Going Global". After the initiative of Chinese culture "Going Global" was proposed, more and more scholars have recognized that the translation of legal classics is not only about rejuvenating our own legal culture and system, but also about creating a fair and objective communication channel for the Chinese and western legal cultures. Thus, the primary task for output translation of Chinese legal classics is to promote excellent legal traditions and culture, claim a place for ancient Chinese legal philosophy and theories in world legal philosophy system and improve the diversity of world legal culture.

2. Principles to Be Followed in Translation of Chinese Legal Classics

(1) Proceeding from China's Specific Situations

In the process of translating Chinese legal classics, the first and the most important principle to be followed is sticking to the actual situations of China. One thing that differentiates culture from civilization is that culture shows the differences and diversities among different nations and represents the personality and characteristics of a nation while civilization reflects the commonality and universality in behaviors and achievements of human beings, which would cause the reduction of ethnic uniqueness (Elias, 2018). The greatest merit of culture is that it can keep the special quality of each and every nation and protect the nation from being assimilated by any other nation.

In the western civilization system, Christianity and modern legal institution are two basic standards for evaluation of a civilization. This system is essentially a system using western culture as a standard to deny the uniqueness and rationality of other nations' cultures. In other words, it is a system aiming at controlling discourse hegemony. Therefore, translators and scholars, when carrying out translation and research of traditional legal classics, must not take versions and results made by western sinologists and scholars as the starting point and base of study or blindly rely on the western theories, methodologies and research paths. Limited by different standpoint and interest needs, we can never use these theories and methodologies to give an accurate and objective description of traditional Chinese legal culture or summarize the basic features of ancient Chinese law. To make a biased conclusion the presumption for translation and study of Chinese legal classics, no wonder the results would be unconvincing. Therefore, one should, when carrying out translation and study of Chinese legal classics, proceed from the ancient judicial practices and actual national situations, examine and rethink the strengths and weaknesses of western theories, innovate and create new theories and methodologies suitable for interpreting and expressing Chinese legal culture.

(2) Jumping out of the Western Discourse System

In the light of present situations, traditional Chinese legal culture has been attached with such conceptual labels as uncivilized and backward by the westerners. This is an image shaped by others instead of ourselves and, of course, it is neither objective nor friendly. Thus, another principle to be observed in translation of Chinese legal classics is breaking the image shaped by the western world and jump out of the established western discourse system. The only way to get rid of the influences of such discourse system is to express concepts in traditional Chinese legal culture in a Chinese way. More specifically, there are three steps to be completed. Firstly, in defining the specific traditional legal concepts, one should pay attention to the differences between traditional legal concepts and the modern ones, fully understand the connotations and denotations of the traditional legal concepts and avoid misperception and misinterpretation resulted from mechanically using modern words and expressions to elucidate traditional legal culture. Secondly, one should give full play to his or her subjective initiative to eliminate the misleading concepts. Thirdly, one should summarize and extract new concepts and new expressions that can truly represent Chinese legal culture upon prudent review of ancient legal practices and careful consideration of Chinese culture and Chinese experiences. If the translators and researchers can finish these three steps flawlessly, it would be much easier to construct our own discourse system and shape a new image of our own legal culture in the international community.

(3) Establishing Self-expression of the Traditional Legal Culture

President Xi Jinping argued that "those who falling behind would be oppressed; those who are in poverty would suffer from starvation; and those who lose the discourse power would be abused" (Xi, 2018). Since we have already solved the first two problems, which are backwardness and poverty, the remaining issue before us is to find effective way to obtaining discourse power in the international community. Thus, in translating and promoting Chinese legal classics, one should follow the principle of establishing self-expression. To tell the story of excellent Chinese legal culture well, accuracy, conciseness and understandability are only the most basic requirements. It should be recognized that there would inevitably be discrepancies in both understanding and judgement. In order to stimulate the audience's interests in Chinese legal culture to the greatest extent and minimize the influences of the audience's inherent biases, one must study the habits and preferences of difference audiences, create new expression methods, and use simple but appropriate expressions to convey the wisdom, ideas and propositions of traditional legal culture. However, the establishment of self-expression is not done for the sake of itself. The main aim thereof is to convey the thoughts behind the expressions efficiently to the audiences, show them what traditional Chinese legal culture real like though refined and wonderful translation, and improve acceptance and identification of Chinese legal system and legal culture among the international community.

3. Implications of Translation of Chinese Legal Classics

(1) Supporting China's Rule-of-Law Construction and Further Improving the Modernization of Rule-of-Law

Speaking of the great rejuvenation of the Chinese nation, the first comes the rejuvenation of culture, which including the rejuvenation of legal culture (Zhang, 2020, 2014). President Xi Jinping once argued that "there is a wealth of wisdom and resources in our ancient legal institution and the Chinese legal system has distinguished itself from other legal systems in the world. We should pay attention to study our ancient legal traditions, learn from the successes and failures of legal practices, explore and inherit Chinese legal culture, assimilate the essence and discard the dregs" (Xi, 2015a, 2015b). The modern legal culture under the socialism with Chinese characteristics have been deeply influenced by traditional legal thoughts and the origins of multiple practices relating to legislation, judicature, law enforcement, and legal supervision can be found in the ancient legal culture (Hu & Dong, 2018a, 2018b). There may be two major advantages for carrying out translation and study of ancient Chinese legal classics. One is that such translation and study can encourage and stimulate current scholars to review and reinterpret excellent legal cultural resources, distill the refined essence of traditional legal culture in a more comprehensive and scientific manner, activate the long dormant Chinese legal system and endow it with new cultural values meeting the needs of the times. Another is that the translation and study of legal classics can effectively eliminate the inadaptability resulted from learning and transplantation of western laws and theories in the modernization of rule-of-law, promote the integration of ancient and modern legal cultural resources, consolidate the historical foundation of rule-of-law construction, and energize the construction of a modern eastern legal system with Chinese characteristics.

(2) Increasing the Public's Confidence in the Nation's Rule-of-Law and Shaping Legal Cultural Identity Both at Home and Abroad

The Chinese legal classics are cultural products in the spiritual dimension, recording and summarizing the experiences and reflections of our ancestors relating to legal practices and social governance. The ideologies, theories, values contained therein shaped how we Chinese people think of fairness and justice, how we value right and wrong and how we judge ourselves. In other words, the Chinese legal classics form the Chinese nation's collective memory of law, of rules and of justice. They are the roots and foundation for Chinese people's confidence in our rule-of-law modernization. Translation is an important tool for acknowledgement, exchange and mutual learning among different cultures and a perfect approach for shaping collective, national or even transnational legal memory. Hence, the translation of Chinese legal classics in the new era will undoubtedly facilitate the spreading of Chinese legal culture in the international community, deepening Chinese people's self-consciousness of and confidence in Chinese legal culture and socialist rule-of-law with Chinese characteristics, and promoting legal cultural identity and acceptance in the international community as well.

(3) Contributing to the Spreading of Chinese Legal Culture and Promoting the "Westward Transmission of Chinese Legal Culture"

Since modern times, numerous people with lofty ideals worked arduously to save the Chinese nation when the very existence was at stake and tried a variety of ways to return this great country to its former glory. On that account, they built up a new modern legal system on basis of western legal thoughts and institutions. Such thoughts and institutions opened up a new world of progressive philosophy of law, inspiring legal values and advanced legal framework for the domestic legal academia, but the influences thereof are so strong that many people start to question the epochal value and historical significance of traditional Chinese legal culture, which greatly hinder the progress of the rejuvenation of the Chinese legal system. Under the excellent historical situation of establishment of socialist legal system with Chinese characteristics, the translation and study of traditional legal classics is an inevitable course if we want to better show the special charms of Chinese legal culture, reverse the stereotyped image of international society toward the Chinese legal system and dispel the long accumulated institutional bias. Further, output translation of Chinese legal classics may also exert positive effects on spreading core values of Chinese legal culture, facilitating the fair communication between the Chinese legal system and other legal systems, gradually realize "westward transmission of Chinese legal culture" in the process of mutual learning among civilizations and ultimately increase China's discourse power in international rule-of-law construction.

4.6 Conclusion

As the only ancient legal system with an uninterrupted history of over 2000 years, the Chinese legal system once dominated the entire Asia and became the indubitable model for legislation and organization of multiple Asian countries, forming a splendid and influential eastern legal culture formidable enough to compete with the Roman legal culture, the dominating legal culture in the western world.

The countless Chinese legal classics recorded the rich experiences and achievements made by our ancestors during the long history of national governance, telling us who we are, what we have and what we should do as a responsible Chinese. Since 1810 when Sir George Thomas Staunton delivered an English version of *Ta Tsing Leu Lee*, the output translation of Chinese legal classics has undergone a tortuous history of over two centuries. However, neither the amount nor the quality of translation and research completed during this period seemed to be satisfactory. It is observed that there still exist certain problems to be solved. For instance, the overwhelming concentration of studies on certain major codes, dominance of research in a single discipline, lack of professional legal classic translation talents and mature talent cultivation mechanism, and otherwise. These problems have hindered the progress of legal classics translation and need to be solved practically and creatively.

All in all, the rejuvenation of Chinese legal system in the new era can never be achieved without the support and nurture of traditional legal culture. The translation of legal classics "shoulders the important burden of memory shaping, promotion and classification of the legal culture" (Hu & Dong, 2020). At the domestic level, translation of legal classics can enrich the research materials of scholars, enabling them to carry out academic innovation from different perspectives. Furthermore, the translation of legal classics can be conductive for popularization of traditional legal culture, deepen the public's awareness and understanding thereof, and enhance their cultural confidence in China's construction of modernized rule-of-law. At the international level, since the legal classics are the first-hand materials for the outer world to access to Chinese legal culture and form perceptions of Chinese rule-of-law, they have contained great legal wisdom with distinguished national features. However, "with regard to the translation and communication of ancient Chinese cultural classics, professional western sinologists have played a leading role while Chinese scholars carried out study and research in this field much later" (Zhang, 2014).

References

Chen, H. (2016). Xi Yuan Ji Lu: The culmination of ancient Chinese medical jurisprudence. *Chinese Rule-of-Law Culture, 6*, 56–59.

Dong, X. (2016). *Research on standardization of Chinese legislative language*. Beijing Jiaotong University Press.

Elias, N. (2018). *Civilization progress: A study on sociogenesis and psychogenesis of civilization* (P. Wang, & Z. Yuan, Trans.). Shanghai Translation Publishing House.

Gong, P. (2004). Sino-West legal communication before nineteenth century. *Jing Ling Law Review, 1*, 46–59.

Hou, W., Zhang, L., & Jia, G. (1997). A brief discussion on characteristics and values of Chinese legal system. *Journal of Northeast Normal University (Social Science), 3*, 57–61.

Hu, B., & Dong, X. (2018a). Paying attention to the research values of English version of *Ta Tsing Leu Lee*. *China Social Sciences Today*. Retrieved November 27, 2018.

Hu, B., & Dong, X. (2018b). Absorbing essence of traditional legal culture and constructing socialist country under rule of law. *Chinese Social Sciences Today*. Retrieved December 12, 2018.

Hu, B., & Dong, X. (2020). Translation of legal classics promoting construction of culture memory. *Chinese Social Sciences Today*. Retrieved March 27, 2020.

Hudson, G. F. (1995). *The Europe and China* (Z. Wang, S. Li, & Y. Zhang, Trans.). Zhonghua Book Company.

Johnson, W., & Li, M. (1984). Legal philosophy in the *Tang Code*. *Pecking University Law Journal, 4*, 37–42.

Li, J., & Dong, X. (2015). The standardization of translation of local rules and regulations and its countermeasures—A research based on translation practice for rules and regulations in Jiangsu Province. *Southeast Academic Research, 5*, 225–233. https://doi.org/10.13658/j.cnki.sar.2015.05.032

Li, X. (2017). Chinese law in the China review and its research value. *Journal of Comparative Law, 2*, 125–134.

Liang, L. (1992). *Traditional Chinese legal culture and legal modernization*. China University of Political Science and Law Press.

Liu, M. (1998). *General annals of Chinese culture: Volume of art and literature*. Shanghai People's Publishing House.

Liu, X. (2015). *Interpretation of Chinese law in the western world: The Chinese repository and westerner's view of Chinese law in 19th century*. Shanghai Sanlian Bookstore.

Qu, W. (2012). Problems of China's legal terminology translation and its reason reflection—A discussion on the standardization of legal terminology. *Chinese Translators Journal, 6*, 68–75.

Qu, W., & Wan, L. (2019). Legal translation in China in the period of the May Fourth Movement: History and its implications for law and translation studies. *Journal of Foreign Languages, 5*, 96–103.

Staunton, G. T. (2015). *Memories of Sir George Thomas Staunton* (W. Qu, Trans.). Shanghai People's Publishing House.

Su, Y. (2003). Another perspective: Study of Chinese legal culture tradition by British and US scholars in modern history. *Global Law Review, 1*, 76–83.

Turner, K., Gao, H., & He, W. (2004). *Recent American academic writings on traditional Chinese law*. Pecking University Press.

Waley, A. (1999). *Laozi*. Hunan People's Publishing House.

Wang, H. (2018). The output tract of translating Chinese legal literature and its enlightenment. *Political Science and Law, 11*, 119–125.

Wu, S. (1994). *Traditional Chinese legal culture*. Pecking University Press.

Xi, J. (2015a). *A speech made by Xi Jinping at the 2nd Meeting of the Fourth Session of the 18th CPC Central Committee*. Retrieved January 5, 2015, from http://theory.people.com.cn/n/2015/0105/c83846-26323829.htm

Xi, J. (2015b). *A speech made by Xi Jinping at the Working Meeting of National Party School*. Retrieved December 11, 2015, from https://www.ccps.gov.cn/zt/xxgcqgdxgzh/ttxw/201812/t20181211_117811.shtml

Xiong, D. (2019, February 12). Practical significance of study on translation and review of legal classics: Implications of English translation of *Ta Tsing Leu Lee*. *China Social Sciences Today*.

Xu, S. (2019). *Conspectus of ancient Chinese legal literature*. Shanghai Ancient Books Publishing House.

Zhang, F., & Ye, S. (2010). On legal translation teaching. *Chinese Translators Journal, 3*, 48–51.

Zhang, J. (2020a). Promoting Chinese legal culture and constructing Chinese legal system in new era. *Contemporary Law Review, 3*, 151–160.

Zhang, S. (2013). Classics: The indispensable origin of legal culture. *The Journal of Jiangsu Administration Institute, 2*, 130–136.

Zhang, W. (1992). Interpretation of legal culture. *Chinese Journal of Law, 5*, 8–12.

Zhang, X. (2014). Foreign sinologists shall be the main body for output translation of Chinese culture. *China & the World Cultural Exchange, 2*, 3–12.

Zhao, C. (2012). Duplicity of legal text translation: Cultural exchange and information leakage—Taking the English version of *Ta Tsing Leu Lee* as an example. *Minority Translators Journal, 2*, 18–23.

Zhao, C. (2014). *A history of English translation of Chinese classics in 19th century*. Shanghai Foreign Language Education Press.

Chapter 5
Translation of Modern Chinese Laws and Regulations

5.1 History of Modern Chinese Laws and Regulations Translation

After the founding of People's Republic of China in 1949, two publishing houses including Foreign Languages Press and New Century Publishing House specialized in translating the Chinese classical books into foreign languages and about 300 books of 43 foreign languages were published from Oct. 1949 to 1965, of which books on laws were very limited (Ma & Ren, 1997).

Since the reform and opening up in 1978, western laws and law books in large volume were introduced into China and at the same time China's laws and regulations were also gradually translated into foreign languages for overseas readers to better get to know about China's modernization of rule of law. In the initial stage, relatively scarce were the laws and regulations translation in China. Originally, the translation of Chinese laws was mostly organized by the Commission of Legislative Affairs of The National People's Congress of the People's Republic of China. For example, there were two English versions of *Marriage Law of the People's Republic of China* adopted on Sep. 10th, 1980 at that time. One was published by Foreign Languages Press in 1982, and the other was compiled by the Commission of Legislative Affairs of The National People's Congress of the PRC and then published by Foreign Languages Press in 1987 (Chen, 1992). In 1985, for the first time, the Commission of Legislative Affairs of The National People's Congress of the People's Republic of China officially launched the translation of laws, and finally published two volumes including *The Laws of the People's Republic of China (1979–1982)* and *The Laws of the People's Republic of China (1983–1986)*, and until 2012 it has presided over the translation of 230 laws including *The Constitution of the People's Republic of China*, and also published 22 successive books of English version of *The Laws of the People's Republic of China* (Qu, 2012).

According to some articles published in the *Chinese Translators Journal* (originally called *Translators Communication*), an authoritative journal on translation in China in the beginning of 1980s, the English version of *The Constitution of the*

X. Dong and Y. Zhang, *Chinese Legal Translation and Language Planning in the New Era*, https://doi.org/10.1007/978-981-19-8448-8_5

People's Republic of China newly adopted on Dec 4th,1982 was simultaneously released along with the Chinese version, and the team of translation was comprised of experts of both law and Chinese, overseas experts and domestic translators (Qiu, 1983), also including the translators from the Ministry of Foreign Affairs and Foreign Languages Press. After several rounds of revision and polishing, the English version was finally published by Foreign Languages Press in 1983. In addition, some nongovernmental organizations, mainly including some media and publishing houses, also actively translated China's laws into English at that time, such as *China Daily*, *Beijing Review*, *Law Press China*, and other press, to publicize China's laws to the world.

In the late 1980s, Legislative Affairs Bureau of the State Council of the People's Republic of China (thereafter called Legislative Affairs Office of the State Council of the People's Republic of China from 1998) also launched the translation of executive regulations, and sorted out and compiled *Laws and Regulations of the People's Republic of China Governing Foreign-related Matters (1949–1990)*, and then it was published by China Legal Publishing House in 1991. From that time on, it became a routine work for Legislative Affairs Bureau of the State Council of the People's Republic of China to compile the latest laws and regulations concerning foreign-related matters every year. Up to 2011, a series of 21 books on *Laws and Regulations of the People's Republic of China Governing Foreign-related Matters* had been compiled by Legislative Affairs Office of the State Council of the People's Republic of China (Zhang, 2011).

After the entry into WTO in 2001, China's communication with the world was becoming increasingly frequent. In accordance with the requirement of WTO, it is a must for every member country to translate its laws into English to improve its judiciary and executive clarity. Then, translating laws had turned into a vital tool for China's participation in government affairs and information publicity, to help overseas persons in China to be more familiar with China's legal construction, and to alleviate international trade conflict and friction. As a result, increasing was the work of laws and regulations translation from then on. Prior to 2001, it was solely in 1999 that China submitted 180 English versions of laws and executive regulations to the working party on the accession of China.

Up till 2002, the laws and regulations translation were mostly finished over national level. In order to meet the demands of entry into WTO, more and more local governments should actively participate in the regulations and rules translation. In 2003, General Office of the State Council of the People's Republic of China issued and promulgated *Notice of Work on the English Translation and Review of Executive Regulations*, which specified the work responsibility, time limitation, organization and funds for translation and review, and also standardized the work procedure. Most importantly, the notice also pressed the local governments and their departments to be responsible for the translation and review of their issued regulations.

After the notice was released, legislative offices from about 28 provinces, autonomous regions and province-level municipalities have established organizations of translation and review of local regulations and rules with professional and full time staff, and legislative offices from about 18 larger municipal governments also joined the same work, for instance, Nanjing, Suzhou, Xuzhou and Wuxi of Jiangsu Province, to name a few.

As a matter of fact, prior to the promulgation of this notice, Shanghai municipal government, as a forerunner, had launched the translation of local regulations and rules earlier, which could be dated back to 1980s (Chen, 2008). For example, during the period from 1988 to 1996, under the cooperation with Shanghai Committee of Foreign Trade and Economic Cooperation, the Legislative Affairs Office of Shanghai Municipal People's Government altogether consecutively translated and published four books entitled *Regulations and Rules of Shanghai Municipality Governing Foreign-related Matters*, consisting of all the regulations and rules concerning foreign matters issued in these 8 years.

2005 witnessed the beginning of translation and review work of local regulations and rules in Jiangsu Province, led by Legislative Affairs Office of People's Government of Jiangsu Province. The Legislative Affairs Office has held provincial sessions for many times to discuss the existing problems in translation, and also invited experts of legal translation from General Office of the State Council to give them some professional advice and guidance. With the concerted efforts, the members of translation and review group have completed the English translation of over 100 local regulations and rules of Jiangsu Province. Both the Chinese and English version of local regulations and rules are publicized through website and printing (Li & Dong, 2015).

All in all, 40 years since the reform and opening up polices implemented in 1978 has seen the rapid increasing need of China's laws and regulations translation. Originally starting from the country level, this work has shifted to the provincial and municipal level and a growing number of personnel, organizations and offices have devoted to the translation work to show China's achievements in reform and opening up and promoting rule of law.

5.2 The Transition of the Significance of Chinese Laws and Regulations Translation

The significance of China's laws and regulations translation is changing along with the times. Considering from the historical process of China's development, we may say that on the whole it can be divided into two distinct phases, namely, relatively passive phase and highly active phase.

For one thing, the relatively passive phase lasts from the reform and opening up policies carried out in 1978 to China's accession into WTO in 2001. After the founding of People's Republic of China, it established diplomatic relation with relatively few countries. In the world's eyes, China was an old, backward and mysterious country, far from the world's civilization. In the initial stage of reform and opening up since 1978, an increasing number of foreigners rushed into China to invest in commerce and do business trade within China. Needless to say, they were eager to get to know about China's laws and regulations to avoid commercial friction and conflict and Hart's safeguard their interests. To meet the basic requirement of the reform and opening up, translation played an important part of transmitting information and legal culture to the foreigners in China.

As a new nation lagging behind the developed countries in the development of rule of law, Chinese were actively devoting themselves to exploring how to govern their country following the rule of law pathway. During the 1990s, under the leadership of the Communist Party of China, China launched an uphill journey to develop law-based governance. Laws and regulations in large number are formulated to guarantee the whole country running under the rule of law with an aim to building a socialist law system with Chinese Characteristics. This long-lasting reform in rule of law primarily started from the field of Chinese-style market economy, and China made a series of prominent achievements in civil law and economic law. In order to be a member of the WTO, China not only had to formulate its laws and regulations according to the international rules to meet the requirement of the world, but also had to translate them into English to make China better known by the world. As rule of law has become a requisite tool for governing modern countries, internationalization of rule of law is also an inevitable tendency for any relatively later development countries. In this process, translation is a bidirectional action which is not only a window for outside world to look into China, but also a bridge for China to go to the world arena. By and large, this was a passive phase in which China was learning from the world and tried to catch up with the developed countries.

Not until 2011 did the country declare that it had initially finished building a socialist law system with Chinese characteristics. We have to admit that the process was also accomplished within the background that China was more open to the world and gradually gained its position in the world along with its rapidly advancing comprehensive national strength, as it is known to us that the GDP of China had surpassed that of Japan ranking as world's No. 2 economy in 2010. With the economical growth, China gradually gained influence and discourse power in the world arena, marching forward to the center of the world platform. And more and more countries diverted their attention to the development of China and wanted to attain more cooperative opportunities with China.

For another thing, the highly active phase starts from the convening of 18th National Congress of the Communist Party of China in 2012. In the same year, white papers of JUDICIAL REFORM IN CHINA (both in Chinese and English version) were promulgated by the Information Office of the State Council of the People's Republic of China, to actively show the achievements of China's reform in judicial system since the founding of New China in 1949, and especially since the reform and opening up policies were introduced in 1978. This was a critical moment representing that China was turning its relatively passive attitude to actively show its national image to the outside world.

As the strategy of Chinese culture "Going Global" was initially put forward in the beginning of the twenty-first century, it also embraced its new phase after the holding of 18th National Congress of the Communist Party of China. In 2013, China's president Xi Jinping proposed the Belt and Road Initiative to promote and expand trade among the countries along the Belt and Road and develop the economic cooperation partnership relation, thereby building a community of shared future featured by mutual political reliance, economic integration and cultural tolerance. Times is constantly changing as China is shouldering more responsibilities in the world. And China is also actively proposing some plans and contributing its wisdom to build the new international order and participating in global governance.

It's worth noting that law-based governance of China, for the first time, was exactly the main theme of the fourth plenary session of the 18th central committee of the communist party of China in 2014. After this session, 7 foreign language versions of *Documents of the Fourth Plenary Session of the 18th Central Committee of the Communist Party of China*, was compiled and published by Central Compilation & Translation Press to the world in 2015. It had fully demonstrated that our Party and national cause had embarked on a new stage and China was increasingly attaching importance to building a rule of law country image to the world. More importantly, it was only by active translation and publicity that could we really enable the international world to know the basic ideal and strategic plan of our comprehensively advancing the law-based governance of China.

Especially when China has entered into a new era, translation, in particular, has been endowed unprecedented significance. At the 19th National Congress of the Communist Party of China on October 18, 2017, Xi Jinping announced to the world that socialism with Chinese characteristics has entered a new era. A new era also witness the new phase of rule of law in China. After so many years of endeavoring, with brand new rule of law ideal of logic power, sound rule of law systems and fresh rule of law practice, China's rule of law in the new era has unfolded to the world the distinctive enchantment of Chinese experience, approach and path. As Xi Jinping pointed out, socialism with Chinese characteristics entering a new era means that the path, the theory, the system, and the culture of socialism with Chinese characteristics had kept developing, which offers a new option for other countries and nations who want to speed up their development while preserving their independence; and it offers Chinese wisdom and a Chinese approach to solve the problems facing mankind (Xi, 2017).

That's exactly the point where translation should undertake its historical and glorious mission. Considering from the perspective of culture communication, the discourse system of one country's legal field can only gain understanding, support and resonance from the foreign public through international communication. Translation is just like a messenger eliminating the cultural gap and linking the disconnected channel in the past, and is nowadays also helping a country to win the discourse power in the world, thereby establishing China's rule of law national image in the world and contributing Chinese wisdom and approach to global governance. As a cross genealogy of law and interlingual interpersonal behavior, China's legal translation, including translating legal ideas and thoughts, legal languages and cultures and legal norms and legal texts, is a pivotal method for our legal discourse system going global (Dong, 2018). As the indispensable part of China's legal discourse, laws and regulations shows what China has achieved in rule of law and represents the results that China has gained in so many years' development, which can also be a kind of experience for the countries from the Third World to draw from.

As Xi Jinping pointed out in his report at 19th CPC National Congress, we will improve our capacity for engaging in international communication so as to tell China's stories well, present a true, multi-dimensional, and panoramic view of China, and enhance our country's cultural soft power. It must be admitted that improving our capacity in international communication of laws and regulations is precisely contributing to enhancing our country's cultural soft power. Therefore, emphasis should be highlighted on the importance of laws and regulations translation to promote Chinese legal discourse going global, which should be uplifted to the height of an important national strategy. And China, first and last, should also adopt a highly active attitude towards publicizing its law culture to the world.

5.3 The Status Quo of the Research on Chinese Laws and Regulations Translation

Prosperous translation research always comes with prosperous translation industry. Contemporary translation field is now on the road to industrialization which can also in turn bring social vigor and resources to the translation. Therefore, translation's participation in social production should be strengthened. It is common sense that theory comes from practice, and the widened and expanded practice is sure to stimulate the thinking of theory and blaze a new trial for theoretical research (Liu, 2005).

Comparatively speaking, western translation theory developed in a more diversified and systematic way than that of China because they had much more mature translation industry. A variety of western schools and theories of translation began to be translated into China from 1980s, widening Chinese horizon of research on translation. However, the introduced theories were mostly inspired and summarized based on literary translation practice. Actually, the initial translation practice within China was also chiefly focused on the literary field and legal translation started relatively late.

In the 1980s, such scarce was the need of translating laws that the related theoretical research was also a rarity. During this period, only several authors and their articles could be found in the *Translators Communication*, and there were few monographs on legal translation prevalent for others' reference. And the only articles could be found mainly probed into the translation of words and especially how to translate the legal terms with Chinese characteristics into English. Meanwhile, there were few scholars engaging in the study of forensic linguistics.

In western countries, however, a large group of scholars, such as Conley, O'Barr, Gibbons, Trosberg, Solan, Shuy, Bhatia, etc., had started early to do research on the legal language and gained numerous achievements in various fields in forensic linguistics. In 1995, The International Association of Forensic Linguists was founded along with its professional journal *Forensic Linguistics* emerging. And a variety of associations including forensic linguistics, legal translation, and court interpretation etc. in many countries were also established in succession (Zhang, 2001).

Starting from 1990s to this day and age, research on legal translation in China was in the process of gradual expansion, which can be by and large divided into four phases on the whole. From 1992 to 1999, to begin with, it was still in its embryo stage. According to some statistics, less than ten articles on legal translation were published annually in domestic journals (Shan & Fan, 2018). In 1999, in the second place, there appeared a slight upward tendency in legal translation research because *Amendment to the Constitution of the People's Republic of China (1999)* was adopted at the Second Session of the Ninth National People's Congress and was promulgated for implementation. It was specified in this amendment that China would promote rule of law and establish a socialist rule of law country, which had triggered Chinese scholars' research on legal translation to better introduce the situation of rule of law development to foreign scholars. During this time, China is also preparing to join WTO, which required that China had to pay more attention to the international rules and to catch up with the international pace of rule of law. Since the accession into WTO from 2001, in the third place, China had to expand its legal communication with the outside world, leading to much increase in laws and regulations translation and its concerning theoretical research. After 2002, there was a substantial increase in legal translation and about 20 articles were published annually. At the same time, universities and colleges in China also paid special attention to the teaching reform and legal English and legal translation research gained more and more popularity. From 2010, in the fourth place, research on legal translation grew in a rapid pace because law-based governance in China had reached a new point. New thoughts and ideas on rule of law, like comprehensively advancing the law-based governance of China, led Chinese people to highlight the complete construction of laws and regulations system. Inevitably, translation and its concerning research prospers with the formulation of laws and regulations in large number. What's more, following the policy of enrollment expansion of postgraduate students, Master's Program of legal translation, especially Master of Translation and Interpreting, began to be established in growing number of colleges and universities, which also promoted the related research on legal translation.

Generally speaking, research on legal translation so far mainly rivets on the micro and meso level of legal language, such as, translation strategy, translation technique, translation principle, and translation approach, etc., which are normally the core research topic and most authors tried to summarize some general rules for legal translation by pointing out the common errors and misunderstanding in the translation practice. In other words, there is still much room for the research transferring into the macro level of legal language. By and large, three obvious phases of changes can generally be found in the specific content of domestic research on legal translation. From 1992 to 2000, the articles primarily discussed legal translation from the linguistic level, especially the words, or rather, legal terms. This phase of translation research was characterized by reflection of the translation experience, faults finding and comparison between Chinese words and English expressions, and the translation approach and strategy were normally the focus (Jin & Hu, 2000; Li, 1994). From 2001 to 2009, more research deeply probed into the specific translation of words and expressions of laws in China. Meanwhile, with the increasing of legal translation practice, more translation cases and samples were available to the scholars for analysis. In addition, after the introduction of western translation theories into China, more and more scholars, not solely confined to the linguistic level, were inspired by western theories and tried to apply them, such as text topology, functional equivalence, skopos theory, and cross-cultural perspective etc., to guide legal translation and their attention was also shifted from legal terms to textual level and text style (Zhang & Zhong, 2005; Lin, 2006; Zhang, 2009), which further widened the research horizon to a high level. From 2010 to now, there is also a growing application of western theories to legal translation research, such as, relevance theory, cooperative principle, etc. Besides, with an increasing number of universities and colleges running new major of legal English or legal translation, more attention was paid to the macro level, that is, the legal translation studies and discipline development gradually caught scholars' eyes. And the laws and regulations translation were in an unprecedented demand compared to that of in the past. The prosperous legal translation industry was also in great demand of related talents. As a result, such words as interdisciplinary talents cultivation gradually became a heated and central topic for cultivating legal English and legal translation talents (Xu & Qu, 2014; Zhang, 2018). Meanwhile, with the rising of translation corporations and enterprises, large number of research entitled translation practice and translation report have emerged. Translation work is gradually considered as projects involving many personnel and procedures, which need much more cooperation and coordination than before. Consequently, professionalization and project management of translation has also been introduced into legal translation research. On the other hand, it was in this stage that legal terminology translation has become the key point for academic research. Along with the normalization and standardization of terminology put forward in all fields of natural and social sciences, the standardization of legal terminology translation also gradually become the more often talked theme n legal translation studies, with their major concern centering on the standardization of legal terminology in national laws and regulations or local regulations and rules translation. It is safe to say that standardization is also a new and ever developing research worthy of much deeper attention.

All in all, academic research in legal translation thrives along with many factors, including China's reform and opening up policies, the prosperous legal translation industry, the much-needed interdisciplinary talents cultivation and active legal translation teaching reform in universities and colleges. Definitely, more and more devotion to translation practice will enrich related theoretical research, and interdisciplinary talents cultivation, as a new research field, also needs more solid theoretical foundation to gain smooth and sound development.

References

Chen, X. (2008). Studies of language standardization concerning C-E translation of local regulations. *Journal of Beijing College of Politics and Law, 4*, 41–61.

Chen, Z. (1992). *Discussion on legal translation.* China Translation Corporation.

Dong, X. (2018). Legal Translation Contributing Chinese Wisdom to Global Governance. *Chinese Social Sciences Today*, June 26, 3.

Jin, C., & Hu, A. (2000). On the existing problems of China's legal translation. *Chinese Translators Journal, 3*, 46–51.

Li, J., & Dong, X. (2015). The standardization of translation of local rules and regulations and its countermeasures—A research based on translation practice for rules and regulations in Jiangsu Province. *Southeast Academic Research, 5*, 225–233. https://doi.org/10.13658/j.cnki.sar.2015.05.032

Li, W. (1994). On the linguistic feature of legal English and its translation. *Chinese Translators Journal, 6*, 15–18.

Lin, W. (2006). On comparative legal culture and legal translation. *Chinese Translators Journal, 3*, 58–63.

Liu, M. (2005). *Translation thinking in China and in the West.* China Translation Corporation.

Ma, Z., & Ren, R. (1997). *History of world's translations of Chinese writings.* Hubei Education Press.

Qiu, K. (1983). On the English translation of some words in the constitution of the People's Republic of China. *Translators Communication, 3*, 15–17+36.

Qu, W. (2012). Problems of China's legal terminology translation and its reason reflection—A discussion on the standardization of legal terminology. *Chinese Translators Journal, 6*, 68–75.

Shan, Y., & Fan, W. (2018). A knowledge mapping analysis of legal translation studies in China (1992–2016)—Based on the 702 research documents of CNKI. *Contemporary Foreign Languages Studies, 4*, 85–93.

Xi, J. (2017). Xi Jinping's report at 19th CPC National Congress. *Xinhuanet*. Retrieved November 3, 2017, from http://www.xinhuanet.com/english/special/2017-11/03/c_136725942.htm

Xu, D., & Qu, W. (2014). Some thoughts on establishing profession certification system in legal translation sector. *Foreign Languages and Their Teaching, 4*, 86–90.

Zhang, C., & Zhong, W. (2005). On the applicability of functional translation theory to legal translation. *Language and Translation, 3*, 44–48.

Zhang, F. (2009). Cultural factors in legal translation. *Chinese Translators Journal, 6*, 48–51.

Zhang, F. (2018). On legal translation teaching and talents cultivation under the belt and road initiative. *Chinese Translators Journal, 2*, 31–35.

Zhang, F. (2011). *On the socialist law system with Chinese characteristics and the achievements of China's laws and regulations translation.* Retrieved September 21, 2011, from http://edu.china.com.cn/2011-09/21/content_23464348.htm

Zhang, Z. (2001). Text type and legal texts. *Modern Foreign Languages, 2*, 191–196.

Chapter 6
Theoretic Framework and Violation of Norms in Laws and Regulations Translation

6.1 Norm Theory: A Theoretical Framework

By norm, according to *Black's Law Dictionary*, it refers to "1. A model or standard accepted (voluntarily or involuntarily) by society or other large group, against which society judges someone or something. 2. An actual or set standard determined by the typical or most frequent behavior of a group" (Garner, 2009). In its definition, norm is explained in two levels, that is, the society and the group, with the central word standard. In effect, as an evolutionary process, both the society and the group can gradually form its own standard of action. By standard, in accordance with *Black's Law Dictionary*, it refers to "1. A model accepted as correct by custom, consent, or authority. 2. A criterion for measuring acceptability, quality, or accuracy" (Garner, 2009). Both definitions of norm and standard can be references for us to have some thoughts on translation. In reality, the study of translation is always in progress, from the initial linguistic level to later societal and cultural level, which is so-called "cultural turn" in western translation theory. In other words, as a human communication behavior, translation is indispensably influenced by the custom, ideology or authority of the certain society. Nowadays, translation work, following the prosperous translation industry, is always done within a group or organization rather than only finished by an individual. As translation industry itself grows mature, the group always voluntarily formulates its criterion or standard for measuring the acceptability, quality or accuracy of translation. All in all, norms of translation can be considered from different levels, or rather, from both the micro and macro level. Such is also the evolution process of the concentration of translation theory.

Actually, norm is a central concept of Descriptive Translation Studies. Representative western scholars like Gideon Toury, Andrew Chesterman, and Theo Hermans, have systematically expounded the norm theory in translation studies. Late 1970s saw the great transition from the prescriptive to descriptive studies of norms in translation. And the units studied ascended from lexical and sentence level to textual and super-textual level, and from linguistic norms to the social and societal norms transcending linguistic category.

X. Dong and Y. Zhang, *Chinese Legal Translation and Language Planning in the New Era*, https://doi.org/10.1007/978-981-19-8448-8_6

In his *Descriptive Translation Studies and Beyond*, Gideon Toury considered translation as a norm-governed activity. As translation inevitably involves two languages and two cultural traditions, the socio-cultural constraints Toury called norms. In terms of the process of translation event, particularly the decision making process, Toury distinguishes two larger groups of norms applicable to translation: preliminary versus operational, involving the selection of text before translation, translation policy and translation decision during the translation (Toury, 2001), but he didn't explore the theoretical side of the norms concept further.

Different from Toury's norm theory, limited to the process of translation, Andrew Chesterman widened the scope of norm theory to social norms, ethical norms and technical norms. Social norms mainly coordinate interpersonal relationship, ethical norms refer to the criterion of values that translators should observe, such as, thoroughness, truth, trusting and understanding, and technical norms mean that translators should meet the expectancy of the readers and comply with the mainstream translation tradition of the target language (Liu, 2009). Based on Toury's research, Chesterman studied norm theory in a more detailed way and put forward his own set of norm theory, consisting of product or expectancy norms and professional norms. Actually, the expectancy norms, as a matter of fact, similar to Toury's preliminary and operational norms, specifically refer to the influencing factors such as translation tradition, discourse convention, and economic and ideological considerations. And professional norms regulate the translation process itself, which can be further divided into three kinds, namely, the accountability norm, the communication norm, and the relation norm. The accountability norm is an ethical one, dealing with professional standards of integrity and thoroughness. The communication norm is a social one, implies that the translator should work to ensure maximum communication between the parties. The relation norm is a linguistic one, which deals with the relation between ST and TT (Chesterman, 1997; Munday, 2001), limited to the translation field. Chesterman proposed relevant similarity to take place of the traditional equivalence relation between the source and target text, with the aim of seeking optimal similarity for translation mission.

Theo Hermans, starting from the perspective of social system theory, attempted to overcome the limitation of the norms research and brought norms to a larger system. According to him, viewing translation as a social system may open up interesting perspectives (Hermans, 2009). Hermans put forward self-reference and heteronomy. Seeking regularity and norms where self-reference really lies in is a must for translation studies itself. However, beyond translation system, translation has to be linked with other systems like ideology, society and culture. Self-reference of translation doesn't mean to be remained rigid and stagnant but refers to the development of regularity of discipline, while heteronomy represents the openness and dynamics of translation studies. Generally speaking, Hermans argues that there are three levels of norms dominating translation, namely, cultural and ideological norms of society, translation norms of conceptual reconstruction of translatability, and the dominant text norms in the particular reader (or client) system.

In general, norm theory in Descriptive Translation Studies, especially Chesterman's classification of norms, has given us operational guidance for reflection on laws and regulations translation in China. Actually, we can study the norms of legal translation from different angles, such as, horizontal and vertical level, or rather, micro (linguistic level) or macro (work mechanism management) level, or from the process of translation like preliminary phase, intermediate phase and post translation phase.

6.2 Violation of Norms in Modern Laws and Regulations Translation

Every industry runs in accordance with its own norms and standardization. Certainly, norms are not built in one day but naturally evolve in a process, interfered by authority and being steered to the virtuous direction. Unavoidably, the thriving laws and regulations translation in China comes along with problems in its not so long history of development. These problems appeared can be called violation of norms in different aspects. As for the macro level of translation management, violation of communication norm, that is, poor coordination and cooperation between different departments, normally can be found. As for micro level in translation itself, violation of accountability norm and relation norm in translators' ability, translation principle, translation quality and so on, also appears. With regard to the process of translation, violation of preliminary norms, such as selection of the appropriate translators, always emerges, involving the cultivation of interdisciplinary talents, especially legal translation talents. And still attention should be paid to the post translation phase, for instance, the standardization work of legal translation and the handling of translation achievements or assets. With the development of new technology, especially the computer-aided translation, technical norm is also a new topic for nowadays translation. In a word, different levels of violation of norms seems to be separate but are unified as a whole in a systematic way.

1. Not Well-formed Working Mechanism

Nowadays, the departments formulating laws and regulations themselves in China are also responsible for their translation. In other words, there are a number of departments and personnel, country level as well as local level, engaging in the laws and regulations translation. To be specific, as for the country's laws and matters concerning the laws, their translation work is organized and reviewed by departments of The National People's Congress of the People's Republic of China; as for the executive regulations promulgated by the State Council of the People's Republic of China, their translation work is organized and reviewed by the Legislative Affairs Office of the State Council; and the translation of local regulations and rules of divisions and departments is organized and reviewed by themselves respectively (Liu et al., 2004). In other words, there are altogether at least three independent forces engaging in the translation work. For the country level, concerning departments have started laws and regulations translation over thirty years and accumulated adequate experiences. With the support from experts of the professional legal field and the renowned publishing houses, the translation quality can be largely secured. However, there can still be some violation of norms in laws and regulations translation, especially the inconsistency of the use of terminology (Fan, 2014). More importantly, numerous problems might have emerged with the surging translation of local legislation.

Normally, scarce communication, or violation of communication norm, is there among the three forces. As a result, the use of terminology and the expressions of concepts is hard to reach consensus precisely because there are wide scope of laws and regulations in China, large number of translators' participation, and many procedures involved etc.… So many departments and personnel will bring numerous problems to communication management, and the fact is that each department even fights his own battle. Different from the literary translation, which admits and invites multi versions of translation, legal translation seeks consistency and accuracy, and the controversy on translation should be unified into one authoritative version to safeguard its authority. Considering from the vertical point of view, the departments from country level are still not communicating enough well with that of the local level, which surely invites a series of problems, for instance, there is inevitable discrepancy of English translation concerning the legal terms between the upper-level legislation (superior legislation) and the lower-level legislation (inferior legislation). As the target readers are all foreigners, the inconsistency among different legal texts are sure to bring misunderstanding, even having a detrimental effect on the whole country's rule of law image.

Furthermore, considering from the horizontal point of view, although over 28 provinces, autonomous regions and province-level municipalities have devoted to regulations and rules translation, their working efficiency and translation quality vary from regions. In advanced regions, particularly for those started earlier in regulations and rules translation, they have, through years of practice, accumulated much experience and formed relatively standardized working procedure, and now are in a leading position in this field. However, for those set out comparatively backward, they are still in the exploration stage with many difficulties to overcome. Obviously, considering from a systematic work including forming a specialized team of translators and establishing a sound working procedure, violation of professional norms facing the translation of some local legislation are diversified, which can be normally summarized as follows.

Firstly, there is uneven level of professional working teams of translators. Currently, modes of translation are distinct from local departments. As previously mentioned, the translation of regulations and rules of local legislation is always done by its Legislative Office of the regional people's government. Noticeably, different are the approaches adopted. Some recruit translators from the graduates of colleges and universities as their full time staff, or even directly appoint staff of their own departments, due to limited funds and support, to finish the translation work. As legal translation is highly professional work, its quality cannot, without specialized experts' guidance, be secured. Others completely leave the tasks to the translation corporations and enterprises. As translation industry in China is also in its phase of initial development, the norms for the whole industry has not been well established, therefore, some translation corporations, free from strict supervision and short of professional translators, seek only for profits and still cannot really be responsible for the quality of translation. Still others which are also of rarity, with adequate funds and support from local governments, have organized a relatively stable team of experts from universities, including professors of both law and foreign languages, specializing in regulations and rules translation (Li & Dong, 2015).

Certainly, a professional team can secure the quality and accuracy of the translation and a stable team can also guarantee the continuity of the whole translation work. As legal translation is a systematic work, a changeable team, on the contrary, tends to bring much trouble. For instance, local regulations and rules are normally formulated according to the upper-level laws and regulations, translators not professional enough will not, when translating local regulations and rules, consult the already translated upper-level legislation, resulting in the discrepancy of terminology between lower-level legislation and upper-level legislation. In addition, the formulation of local regulations and rules is a systematic work and there are also close relation between them. The consistency should also be guaranteed when we translate local regulations and rules. Inevitably, constantly changing translators will also disconnect the continuity of the translation of related regulations and rules, in other words, the same terminology might, caused by the knowledge and understanding of different translators, have different translation in related regulations and rules. Even in the same regulations or rules, there might be inconsistency for the certain terminology because of the poor communication among the team and bad procedural management of the whole translation work.

Secondly, there is uneven level of team management. Different from the past translation practice, modern translation is always characterized by heavy workload, team cooperation and short time limitation etc. Since translation is no longer done by single handed person, there should be good organization and coordination among the whole team. Considering from the workload, certainly, the relatively less translation work could still be finished by individuals. However, in light of the increasing volume of local legislation, it is necessary to pay more attention to team management. Nowadays, much as some local legislative affairs offices have organized a work team, they don't manage it well and even there is no real cooperation and coordination between translators. Some just finish the task without the procedure of proofreading and reviewing. There are only a few who can not only provide adequate money and professional translators but also have set up the formal translation management procedure.

2. Inadequate Cultivation of Interdisciplinary Legal Translation Talents

Legal translation is oriented to the elite group which is of high quality and technical difficulty. Specifically speaking, legal translation serves the social upper-level groups such as lawyers, foreign invested enterprises, and import and export corporations, with extremely high requirement of accuracy of translation. Certainly, accurate translation at the same time means relatively high technical difficulty. In a sense, legal translation talents are also elite groups in the society (Dong, 2016). Legal translation is not only doing translation, but also translating laws. In other words, legal translators should be bilingual experts in cross disciplines, that is, linguistics, laws and translation.

As the preliminary norms, selection of the proper translators is the top priority for laws and regulations translation. However, as a new field, legal translation and its talent cultivation are still in its initial stage because only a small fraction of universities and colleges have began to give legal translation courses and few have established the related major and discipline in legal translation, in other words, the cultivation of interdisciplinary legal translation talents is also in its preliminary phase. Taking Jiangsu Province for example, there are altogether 134 universities and colleges within the whole province, of which only several comprehensive universities like Nanjing University, Southeast University, Nanjing Normal University and Soochow University offer the major of translation and only Nanjing Normal University, in particular, offers the teaching of legal translation. As translation discipline in China is also a new one with only a history of over 30 years, and it hasn't formed a system of its own and translation teaching is only small part of the foreign languages education in China. Legal translation, as an interdisciplinary subject, is also a new discipline which needs more time to become mature. Starting later than other translation teaching for specific purposes, legal translation teaching is still confronted with the basic problems such as "what to teach" and "how to teach", without ripened answers. Correspondingly, there are also relatively less research results in the talents cultivation of legal translation (Zhang, 2018a, 2018b) and legal translation teaching (Chen & Deng, 2015).

Currently, the problems facing the legal translation are various, including teaching practice being free from scientific guidance, the inappropriate arrangement of legal translation teaching content and courses leading to students' lack of professional knowledge of law and law culture, weak faculty failing to meet the requirement of the urgent needs, and the outdated teaching methods (Zhang & Ye, 2010). All in all, the cultivation of legal translation talent is falling behind the practical legal translation practice. Those who are skilled at linguistics, translation and law at the same time are necessarily rare and precious ones. As translation is a cross culture activity, legal translation is certainly a cross legal culture activity. Different from Anglo-American law system, China is a country of continental law system and is also under the influence of traditional Chinese legal system. Although there are common things between the two law systems, more are the difference with distinct languages and terms and expressions. Ineligible is the translator who fails to understand the difference and master the knowledge of comparative law. It is a pity that cultivation of qualified legal translation talents is still in its elementary stage, far falling behind market needs. Unavoidably, there has appeared much violation of norms in legal translation because the translators are short of knowledge of the law.

3. Unsystematic and Unsustainable Standardization Work

Standardization invariably comes later than the prosperous industry. Such was also the case in the laws and regulations translation. In general, the standardization of translation has way lagged behind what we have achieved in translating laws and regulations.

Although the concerning departments started the laws and regulations translation from the late 1980s, they just released the standardization results in the 1990s. In 1998, Department of Translation, Review and Foreign Affairs of Legislative Affairs Office of the State Council of the People's Republic of China formally published *Legal Words and Expressions (Chinese & English): A Handbook for the Translation of Laws and Regulations of People's Republic of China* (thereafter short for *Handbook*, published by China Legal Publishing House). In 2005, it also compiled and printed *Legal Structures: A Handbook for the Translation and Review of Regulations* (thereafter short for *Handbook*), but this handbook was not formally published and merely for internal references (Qu, 2012). Upon its publication and publicity, the handbook had become the authority guidance and the necessary reference book for the translators of translating local regulations and rules.

Since the 2000s, Legislative Affairs Office of the local governments also joined the standardization of translating regulations and rules. As the pioneer, Department of Translation, Review and Foreign Affairs of Institute of Executive Legislative of Legislative Affairs Office of the People's Government of Shanghai Municipality also released its achievements in standardization of regulations and rules translation. The standardized legal terms were released in the journal entitled *Translating Regulations* (not formally published, founded in 2002, as quarterly printing), in which there was a column named standardization of translation, as the core content. As the forerunner in translating regulations, Shanghai's standardization of translation also established certain authority, with its results reposted by Legislative Affairs Office of the State Council of the People's Republic of China on its official website.

Since the beginning of translating regulations and rules, Legislative Affairs Office of the People's Government of Jiangsu Province also attached the importance of standardization. As far as standardization, the mechanism and the quality of translation are concerned, Jiangsu province is now relatively in the lead throughout the country, and had been commended for several times by the State Council of the People's Republic of China (Dong, 2016). After over ten years' translation practice, it had become a voluntary consciousness for Jiangsu Province to launch the standardization. In order to secure the accuracy of translation to improve the quality, with the concerted efforts, the members of the translation group actively extracted the high frequency terms and habitual use of structures from large volume of translated texts. In 2018, the translation group compiled and printed its standardization achievements entitled *Legal Terms and Structures: A Handbook for the Translation of Regulations and Rules of Jiangsu Province* (not formally published). In this handbook, 3000 habitual terms and 90 structures have been selected for translators' references, thereby becoming a handbook for those translating local regulations and rules (Legislative Affairs Office of the People's Government of Jiangsu Province 2018).

Although certain achievements have we gained in the standardization work, this accomplishment, however, on the whole, is unsystematic and unsustainable. For one thing, standardization itself should be a systematic work. With translation merging in large scale and complication, merely dependent on the several translators of high capability is far not enough to meet the actual requirement. On the contrary, the work should be done in a project with overall planning, specific service program, qualified language resources and appropriate service forms. Under this circumstance, the professional management is of paramount importance (Wang & Wang, 2012). Or rather, the standardization work of translation has been further expanded, from the micro level to the macro level. However, the current standardization is still confined to the linguistic level, far from the systematic requirement.

For another thing, standardization itself should be a sustainable work. From the national level, after the *Handbook* in 1998 and 2005 were released by the Legislative Affairs Office of the State Council of the People's Republic of China, there have been no other new results in the standardization up till now. As for the local endeavoring, the journal *Translating Regulations* compiled by Shanghai was also discontinued, and there have been no new achievements since the 2011. Over ten years, great changes have taken places in China, and still ongoing is the laws and regulations translation. More and more departments and personnel have devoted to this field with increasing number of laws and regulations being translated into English and publicized to the foreigners. On the one hand, laws and regulations run within the social environment which constantly changes with the times. Both national and local legislation have to respond to the social development and change in an active, flexible and rapid way. Times changes, and such is the repeal and amendment of laws and regulations which are out of fashion. Furthermore, more and more local governments have been entrusted the power of legislation. Relatively different from the central legislation of country level, the local legislation bears the value of relative independence, or rather, without running counter to *The Constitution of the People's Republic of China*, current laws and executive regulations, local legislation has the right to, in accordance with the specific situation and actual requirement of the local regions, autonomously handle local affairs and formulate regulations and rules featured by the local characteristics. As China is a large country, the situation and social development vary from one local region to another (Tian, 2004). With new laws and regulations emerging, their translation is also a nonstop work. In other words, the standardization should not be a contemporary but a permanent work along with the translation practice to secure the translation quality.

4. Not Sound Integration of Translation Practice and Research

For a long time, the separation of practice and research exists in China's translation circle, leading to the ineffective application of the translation theory to translation practice (Du et al., 2004). Up till now, scholars largely from the school of foreign languages and cultures of colleges and universities have devoted to the legal translation studies. Though some of them also engage in translation practice, as a matter of fact, more complex is the combination of legal translators, of which some are from translation corporations and some from the legislative affairs office of the local governments. To be specific, a lot of articles and books have talked about the principle of legal translation. And there are also articles discussing the principle of terminology translation. In these articles, the principles are always summarized by words, for example, normalization, accuracy, equivalence, consistency, and professionalism etc. Certainly, these words are of conciseness and simplicity, which are suitable for being the principle of legal translation but far from concrete operational approaches. In practice, every translator has his own understanding of legal translation. Without the academic training as scholars from universities, not every translator can really read these articles and strictly follow these principles. On the other hand, the practical translation is more complicated. China's written laws and regulations are various, for instance, as for the names, there are over 30 kinds in laws and executive regulations with diversified English translation (Zhang, 2018a, 2018b). Different translators tend to choose different English words and expressions for even the same terminology. Currently, a situation of "Hundred Schools of Thoughts" has emerged in China's legal translation because there is short of unity in the translation of legal terms and sentences (Wang, 2015).

At the same time, it is hard to form a systematic translation theory. As legal translation is a highly practical work, the current research mostly centers on translation principle, translation approach and translation strategy to directly serve the translation practice. Considering from the current research results, the concerning theoretical research, comparatively speaking, was relatively weak and is worthy of being strengthened. Or rather, it is obvious that there is less research talking about the problems in legal translation from the translation theory. Theoretical research, solid or not, directly determines the development room and depth of the discipline. However, what we can find now mostly is the descriptive summary of translation examples or the explanation of the author's reflection. The lack of theoretical research gives neither definite methodology nor clear aims for deep research on legal translation. Distinct from the literary translation, legal translation research should also have its own theoretical foundation with distinctive style.

References

Chen, Q., & Deng, L. (2015). A study of the implementation model of genre-based pedagogy in legal translation teaching. *Journal of Guangdong University of Foreign Studies, 5*, 24–29.

Chesterman, A. (1997). *Memes of translation: The spread of ideas in translation theory*. John Benjamins Publishing Company.

Dong, X. (2016). *Research on standardization of Chinese legislative language*. Beijing Jiaotong University Press.

Du, J., Zhang, F., & Yuan, L. (2004). Problems of English translation of China's laws and regulations and their solution. *Chinese Translators Journal, 3*, 74–78.

Fan, H. (2014). Major mistakes in the English translation of general principles of the civil law of the People's Republic of China. *4*, 88–91.

Garner, B. A. (2009). *Black's law dictionary* (9th ed.). A Thomas Reuters Business.

Hermans, T. (2009). *Translation in systems: Descriptive and system—Oriented approaches explained*. Routledge.

Legislative Affairs Office of the People's Government of Jiangsu Province. (2008). *Legal terms and structures: A handbook for the translation of regulations and rules of Jiangsu Province.*

Li, J., & Dong, X. (2015). The standardization of translation of local rules and regulations and its countermeasures—A research based on translation practice for rules and regulations in Jiangsu Province. *Southeast Academic Research, 5,* 225–233. https://doi.org/10.13658/j.cnki.sar.2015.05.032

Liu, J. (2009). *A central history of western translation theory.* Wuhan University Press.

Liu, Z. (2004). Stratification Study of Social Forms and Discussion on Ruler's Dominance over Society, *Historical Research, 2,* 9–16.

Munday, J. (2001). *Introducing translation studies: Theories and applications.* Routledge.

Qu, W. (2012). Problems of China's legal terminology translation and its reason reflection—A discussion on the standardization of legal terminology. *Chinese Translators Journal, 6,* 68–75.

Tian, C. (2004). *Theory and practice of regional legislation.* China Legal Publishing House.

Toury, G. (2001). *Descriptive translation studies and beyond.* Shanghai Foreign Language Education Press.

Wang, H., & Wang, H. (2012). *A practical guide to translation project management.* China Publishing & Media Holdings Co., Ltd. & China Translation Corporation.

Wang, W. (2015). Analysis on disunity in the English versions of the Chinese laws and regulations. *Journal of Jiangxi Normal University (Philosophy and Social Sciences Edition), 5,* 137–139.

Zhang, F. (2018a). On legal translation teaching and talents cultivation under the belt and road initiative. *Chinese Translators Journal, 2,* 31–35.

Zhang, F., & Ye, S. (2010). On legal translation teaching. *Chinese Translators Journal, 3,* 48–51.

Zhang, Q. (2018b). A study on the English translation of the names of Chinese laws and regulations. *Journal of Zhejiang Gongshang University, 1,* 29–33.

Chapter 7
A Case Study: Translation of Legal Terms

7.1 Introduction

Legal translation in modern times has made great changes to China's thousands of years of feudal legal traditions and the legal system of Chinese vocabulary. This great achievement, together with its significant contributions, deserves all the praises from scholars in laws, grammar study, and especially specialists in translation (Xiong, 2010). It is believed among scholars that every single legal term clearly and relevantly speaks for a specific legal norm of conduct, and therefore, its unique connotation determines its accuracy, which, becomes a key element affecting the exchanges of legal literature (Liu, 2010). Due to the differences between English and Chinese genealogy of law and legal systems, translators of legal terms may encounter untranslatable or incomplete equivalence. Sometimes the translation may be ambiguous because of polysemy of the term or translator's ignorance of the law of the target country. Therefore, in the translation of English and Chinese legal terms, the translator should not only consider the basic principles of translation of legal documents and some relevant factors, but also clarify the differences between different legal systems and institutions, and flexibly use appropriate translation methods according to the degree of equivalence.

7.2 The Concept and Characteristics of Legal Terms

The so-called legal terminology is used to accurately express some specific legal concepts. According to their usage, legal terms generally can be divided into two categories: One is legal term of art dedicated to the field of legal affairs. Such specialized legal terms are small in numbers and have specific meaning and scope of application, but they cannot be replaced by other word or be arbitrarily extended. Such as: infringement, limitation of action, suspension of execution, the burden of proof, etc.

X. Dong and Y. Zhang, *Chinese Legal Translation and Language Planning in the New Era*, https://doi.org/10.1007/978-981-19-8448-8_7

The other type expresses specific legal concepts, but with the expansion of the scope of application and the mutual influence due to the close exchange of universal vocabulary, those terms which originally were only understood by legal workers now have extended to the universal vocabulary field, such as: lawyers, debt, murder, crimes, prisons, courts, contracts, wills, fines, penalties, judgments, robberies, thefts, acts, signatures, certificates, insurance, marriage, divorce, etc. Legal terminology, like any other subjects, is a professional jargon and a social dialect that makes legal language more accurate, more explicit, and makes communication between legal practitioners more comfortable. Legal terms generally have the following characteristics:

1. The Meaning of Legal Terms Is Professional

Legal terminology is the core part of the legal system, and it's fixed down after the use of a long period of time in the gradual precipitation. A term may mean a legal concept (such as "object", "legal person", "person having no capacity for civil conduct" etc. in civil law), or a legal system (such as "consideration", "estoppel", etc.), or even is associated with special historical background (such as "sealed contract"), the meaning of which cannot be understood solely from the literal words it constitutes (Xiao, 2001).

2. The Meaning of Legal Terms Is Exclusive

In general, after the formation of the legal terms, there will be a specific group of users and a relatively fixed meaning, and therefore, they have certainty in forms. Even if some of the terms are not very accurate during their formation, if its meaning has been well known, they should not be arbitrarily changed. In other words, the meaning of legal terms must be unique and fixed. Any people under any circumstances should have the same interpretation. For example, in Chinese, "故意 (intentional)" cannot be replaced by "存心 (consciouly)" or "特意 (deliberately)", and "犯罪嫌疑人 (suspect)" cannot be replaced by "犯罪可疑人 (criminal suspicious man)". In English, "negligence" cannot be replaced by "mistake"; "uncompleted murder" cannot be replaced by "failure in murder". Not only legal terms require a unique meaning, the legal terms which are transformed from the national common language must also express a unique legal concept.

3. The Meaning of Legal Terms Is Conservative and Authoritative

The meaning of legal terms is conservative and authoritative. Compared with general language, the meaning of legal terms is relatively stable, accurate, and with small changes, which is to reduce the arbitrary application of law, and to achieve social justice. The ancient Chinese words, such as "刑罚 (criminal punishment)" and "自首 (surrender)", are mainly classical Chinese words. These ancient Chinese words and expressions still exist in the real world through historical process. They are inherited as the legal culture of human beings. In the English legal terms, there are a large number of ancient words derived from the Old English and Middle English periods.

Their sources are composed of two parts, some from French, Latin and a small number of Greek and other foreign words, such as "suit", "testimony" and so on.

7.3 Problems Encountered in Translation of Chinese Legal Terms

With the deepening of reform and opening up, China is increasingly participating in international political, economic, and cultural communications. As an important part of legal communication, legal translation has played an indispensable role in the process of globalization. In recent years, remarkable achievements have been accomplished in translation of modern Chinese laws and regulations. However, there are still some problems to be addressed in the translation of legal terms, which are listed as follows.

1. Taking Legal Terms Literally

The translation of legal terms involves dealing with the relationship between popularization and terminology of legal terms. Terminology, also known as theorization, refers to the essential features of the alleged legal things (phenomena) that are revealed in the naming and selection of legal terms, which can reflect the legal concept and theory. In 1998, the People's Republic of China published the Chinese-English Laws and Regulations Vocabulary Handbook, which translated "物证" into "material evidence". In this translation, the "物 (thing)" literally corresponds to "material" in English, while the "证 (evidence)" matches the "evidence". This translation seems correct, but in fact the meaning of its expression is far from the meaning to be expressed. According to the *Black's Law Dictionary (7th edition)*, the interpretation of the term "material evidence" actually means "evidence having some logical connection with the consequential facts or the issues". It may be both verbal evidence and physical evidence. The "物证" in Chinese has a special corresponding legal term in English, which is "real evidence". Therefore, the word "material" in "material evidence" does not mean "material" but means "(the evidence) that is case-related and is necessary and very important in order to prove the truth of the case". It is in this sense that the translation of "material evidence" should be "实质性证据 (substantial evidence)" (Dong, 2011).

Another example is that some translators use "the third party" to translate "第三者 (the third person who steps into other's marriage)" in Chinese legal terms. In fact, "the third party" refers to "第三方, 第三人 (the client involved in the civil action that is outside of the accuser and the defendant and considers that the outcome of the case has an interest in itself and is therefore applied by the court or added to the lawsuit between the accuser and the defendant)". However, "第三者" in Chinese refers to the intervention, interference and destruction of the legal marriage of others, either male or female; both married or unmarried (Chen, 2000).

2. Lacking Understanding of the Legal Cultures and Linguistic Features, Confusing One Legal Term with Another

For example, China's criminal law illegalizes the intrusion into others' houses. How to translate it into English? The English word "burglary" has a meaning of "breaking and entering of the dwelling house of another person", then some translators have the "非法侵入住宅罪 (crime of illegal intrusion into a house)" in our criminal law translated as "burglary", without knowing that the objective aspect of burglary is the perpetrator commits theft after prying the window into the room with a knife, which, is quite similar to the crime of theft in our country.

Article 5 of the Law of the People's Republic of China on Chinese-foreign Equity Joint Ventures stipulates that foreign joint venturers shall compensate for loss or losses if they intentionally deceive through backward technology and equipment and afterwards cause loss or losses. In some English translations this is translated as: "If it causes losses by deception through the intentional use of backward technology and equipment, the foreign joint venture shall pay compensation for the losses."

The translator in this version did not carefully consider the meaning of "loss" in numbers; they ignored the differences between the Chinese and English language, and simply translated as "loss". We know that there is no distinction of singular and plural forms in Chinese, whereas it's quite obvious in English. "损失 (loss)" is both singular and plural in Chinese. Therefore, it is necessary to use "loss or losses" or briefly "loss(es)" in English where singular and plural forms are both possible (Li & Zhang, 2006).

3. Lacking Emphasis on Standardization of Translation, Misunderstanding the Connotation of Legal Terms

Some translators interpret the same legal concepts in Chinese texts in many different English legal terms. For example, the English version of the *Copyright Law of the People's Republic of China* has the act "侵犯" translated into "prejudice" (e.g. Article 12) and "infringe" (Article 48). However, according to the meaning and examples of many English dictionaries, the emphasis of "infringe" is on violations of rights, whereas "prejudice" is more on the violation of people, things and their interests. An example of the use of the word "infringe" is found on page 549 in Modern Advanced English-Chinese Dictionary, Oxford University Press, 1978. It is quoted as "infringe a rule (an oath, copyright, a patent)". From the usage of the term, "infringe" is mainly associated with the "right" in the sense of intellectual property rights. The example of the use of the word "prejudice" on page 826 in the dictionary refers to an infringement of "any existing right or claim". It can be seen that "infringe" is more purposeful in meanings, mainly refers to the violation of intellectual property rights, whereas "prejudice" is a more general meaning, referring to the violation of people, things and interests in any sense whatsoever.

In terms of the translation of "连带责任" and "共同责任", in accordance with the relevant provisions of the *Civil Code*, "连带责任" refers to the joint implementation of two or more people conducting offenses and all have fault, and they should jointly bear the responsibility for the consequences of damage. There are two kinds of joint responsibility: joint liability and shared responsibility. Joint liability arises from the violation of related debt or joint acts of tort, where there is joint relationship between those who shoulder responsibilities. This joint liability is a statutory duty, which cannot be changed due to people's internal agreement, and the obligees can choose either all or part of the people liable to undertake the due obligations, and every people liable is likely to assume full responsibility. However, there is no joint liability between those people liable if they bear the shared responsibility independently. If the law does not stipulate or the parties do not agree, it is presumed that the people liable should bear the same share. Therefore, "连带责任" should be translated as "joint and several liability"; "共同责任" should be translated as "joint liability".

7.4 Potential Strategies and Methods for Translation of Chinese Legal Terms

Susan Sarcevic pointed out in his book *New Approach to Legal Translation* that legal translation is not only the process of language conversion, but a communicative activity conducted under legal mechanism. Legal terms can be divided into three categories: near-equivalence, partial equivalence, and non-equivalence (Sarecvic, 1997). Legal translation, like other translations, is a communicative activity (Du, 2004). However, legal translation is different from other translation in terms of one of its significant features: operability; that is, in cross-legal communication, translators should not only operate in the language level, but more importantly, they should have a clear understanding of the legal culture and legal statute which are not represented simply from words. In the translation of legal terms, we must first study the meaning of the source legal terms to be translated, compare the legal system involved, and try to find the target term with the same content. The selection of the target term should be decided according to the degree of correspondence in which the source language and its target language share, given full consideration of their language functions and legal functions. The more specific classifications of the corresponding terms are as follows:

1. Using Exact Equivalents Where the Legal Concepts Are Equivalent

It is a fact that we translate legal texts between different legal traditions and legal systems, and we have been doing so for the past few centuries. Assisted by the process of translation, the laws and legal systems in many countries and regions have been developed on the basis of legal transplant from other legal familied. Many foreign legal terminologies, concepts, practices have been introduced to China in this way. Therefore, successful experiences tell us that translating legal terms, irrespective of what legal families are involved, is not only possible, but also highly productive. Therefore, in the English translation of Chinese legal terms, where exactly equivalent terms in the English context can be found, the translators can adopt such equivalents to translate the Chinese legal terms. This kind of legal terms are easy to translate; we only have to give one-to-one correspondence between the target words and source words. Such as "court-法庭", "suspect-犯罪嫌疑人", "action-诉讼", "will-遗嘱", "party-当事人", "arbitration-仲裁", and so on.

2. Using Functional Equivalence Where the Legal Concepts Are Partly Equivalent

Sarcevic (1997) argues that functional equivalence is used only when there is no exact equivalence. The so-called functional equivalence words refer to the concept of "the shared function of a particular concept in the legal system between the target language and the source language". By choosing the nearest functional equivalence words, we can ensure that English and Chinese legal terms can obtain relatively accurate translation when there is no exact equivalence word. The choice of the target equivalence word depends on whether the function is equivalent in terms of the concept of the target language and the source language. In other words, whether the legal effect is equal. For example, should the word "mortgage" be translated as " 按揭" or "抵押"? In the legal sense, the difference between "mortgage" and "pledge" lies in the debtor's possession of the real estate. According to *Black's Law Dictionary* (2004), mortgage: A conveyance of title to property that is given as security for the payment of a debt or the performance of a duty and that will become void upon payment or performance according to the stipulated terms. The chief distinction between a mortgage and a pledge is that by a mortgage the general title is transferred to the mortgagee, subject to be revested by performance by of the condition; while by a pledge the pledger retains the general title in himself, and parts with the possession for a special purpose. By a mortgage the title is transferred, by pledge, the possession.

In fact, it can be seen that the connotation of mortgage refers that the property of the real estate will be transferred by the real estate mortgagors to creditors to guarantee the debt, and the debtor is still in possession of the real estate. This is different from the concept of pledge in China's mainland civil law system. According to Article 179 of the *Property Law of the People's Republic of China*, the creditor's rights in general refers to the creditor's right to change the disposition of mortgaged property and the priority to receive compensation when the obligor fails to perform the debt or when the parties realize the mortgage according to their agreement. Therefore, the translation into "按揭" is closer to the legal functional equivalence.

Another example is the term "混合过错 (mixed fault)" in Chinese tort law, which refers to the occurrence or expansion of the damage caused by the tort. In this situation, not only the perpetrator is in fault, but also the victim. "混合过错" is also called "过失竞合". Article 131 of the *General Principles of Civil Law of the People's Republic of China* stipulates explicitly the liability in mixed fault: "The infringer's civil liability can be reduced when the victim should also be responsible for the damage". The legal terminology of the infringing mistake in Anglo-American law system is contributory negligence and comparative negligence. According to The *Free Dictionary of Legal Terms*, "*contributory negligence*" refers to "a doctrine of common law that if a person was injured in part due to his/her own negligence (his/her negligence contributed to the accident), the injured party would not be entitled to collect any damages (money) from another party who supposedly caused the accident" while "*comparative negligence*" refers to "a rule of law applied in accident cases to determine responsibility and damages based on the negligence of every party directly involved in the accident".

Thus, in Anglo-American law system, contributory negligence is due to the victim's fault, and the infringer does not bear civil liability; comparative negligence is decided according to the proportion of the victim's and infringer's civil liability. It is doubtless that comparative negligence is consistent with China's Civil Law General Provisions and judicial practice in that they both partially exempt the infringer's civil liability when "混合过错 (mixed fault)" occurs.

3. Using Flexible Methods When Concepts Are Totally Inequivalent

Where no equivalent can be found in English legal context, the following methods may be adopted to translate this kind of Chinese legal terms:

(1) Paraphrase

The judicial system of Anglo-American law system is very complex and is very different from our judicial system. Many judicial terminologies can't be understood without interpretation. Paraphrasing is to use the neutral language in target language to express the intention and meaning of source language, which is an effective solution to the lack of accurate words. For example, the term magistrate in the United Kingdom is interpreted in the dictionary as "a civil officer administering the law, esp. an official conducting a court for minor cases and preliminary hearings: a Justice of the Peace". Generally the English-Chinese dictionary translates the word as "地方行政官". This concept is obscure for Chinese readers because there is no such concept of "治安法官" in the Chinese legal system. Public security organs are responsible for public security cases in China. Any violation of the Public Security Administration Punishment Law should be dealt with by the public security organs (the police), rather than through the court proceedings. There is "magistrate court" in the British judicial system, so there is a so-called "治安法官", and the judge of the case is called "治安法官 (magistrate)". Translating magistrate into a "审理治安案件的法官 (judge of public security cases)" in the legal context, makes the concept clearer and more accurate by paraphrasing (Bao, 2011).

The use of paraphrase will allow the target readers to better understand a more accurate meaning of the original term, rather than just stay in the literal level, thus improving its readability. For example, "钓鱼执法 (fishing law enforcement)" is a newly emerged legal vocabulary, which refers to a non-normal means, driven by economic interests, to induce law-abiding citizens to break the law, so as to conduct an economic punishment. By using paraphrase, "钓鱼执法" can be translated as: for the economic interest, the law enforcement officials entrap law abiding citizens to break laws and impose a fine.

(2) Using Neutral Terms

Since each and every legal culture possesses its own unique features, some concepts and principles involved in many English legal terms do not exist in Chinese, and it's not likely to find the exact equivalent or nearly equivalent terms. In this case, the translator can translate into neutral words which are non-legal terms after thoroughly understanding the meaning of English legal terms. For example, there is a legal term "fault" in Roman law, which is the obligation of guarantee that the seller must bear in promise contract (contractus consesu). In the past, this legal term has been translated as "xiaci (flaws)" in China, but because it is not common enough, it is now generally translated as "缺陷 (defects)". In Anglo-American law system, libel and slander are tort law concepts rather than criminal law concepts, for the victim can file a claim for damages if there is infringement of reputation. In China, the infringement are regulated by the civil law and criminal law respectively according to its severity, so there is libel. But "libel" and "slander" are not functional equivalences. If the translators use the neutral words "written libel" and "oral defamation", the translation is more appropriate, and can avoid confusion and misunderstanding as well (Tan & Xiang, 2012).

(3) Borrowing

Legal translation is a process of legal communication, legal transplantation and legal development. Chinese legal terms are also enriched in the process of translation. During this process, the method of borrowing has contributed a lot. Before the reform and opening up, China's laws, especially laws and regulations in civil affairs, maritime affairs, environmental protection, marriage and family affairs, etc. are particularly weak. In order to improve China's socialist legal system, many foreign legal terms, such as "动产 (movable property)", "收养 (adoption)", "血亲 (cognation)", etc. in Roman Law were borrowed to China. The most typical is that the "法人 (legal person)" in the civil law, which refers to "organizations with rights and enforcement capabilities, independently enjoying civil rights and assuming civil obligations, including enterprises and institutions, organs and social groups".

It should be noted that due to the large differences in pronunciation and semantic meanings between English and Chinese words, the borrowed English words have to undergo "naturalized" treatment after entering the Chinese legal contexts; that is, some slight changes in pronunciation or semantic meanings have to be made, to make them closer to the Chinese native words. For example, anti-trust law is better translated as "反垄断法" rather than "反托拉斯法".

(4) Neologism

The concept of English and Chinese legal terms is often unequal or even completely unequal. When the use of paraphrase, neutral and borrowed words in translation is difficult to achieve functional equivalence, the corresponding neologisms should be created as new legal terms. For example, "婚内强奸罪 (marital rape)" can be generated because feminists in western countries, such as Britain and the United States, advocate the emancipation of women's personality. But this concept is not found in Chinese law. The Anglo-American law system is very concerned with the judicial proceedings, and therefore many of the concepts in the proceedings cannot be found in our judicial system, such as "辩诉交易 (plea bargain), 辩诉协议 (plea agreement) (referring to the plea bargain agreement that is approved by the court, and is reached by the defendant with the accuser to escape from heavier penalties).

As a result of unbalanced economic development, the asymmetry of financial, securities, insurance and bill legal terms are particularly obvious. For example, " 年金支付通知 (pension warrants), 认股权证书 (share warrants), 职工忠诚保险 (fidelity insurance)", etc. are the result of neologism.

The creation of neologism should reflect the updated spirit and reveal the essential characteristics of the alleged legal things (phenomenon). We should pay attention to the aggregation and systematicness of semantics when creating the terms. For example, the legal term "成年人 (adult)" appeared earlier in our legal system. The term minor/infant was originally translated as "青少年 (adolescent)", "未成年人 (minor child)", etc., but is now generally translated as "未成年人 (juvenile)" because this legal term is symmetrical with the semantic meaning of "成年人 (adult)", so it's easy to understand and master, which embodies the systematic nature of legal terms and the dignity of law.

7.5 Conclusion

One of the difficulties of legal translation is the understanding and expression of legal terms. Because of the difference of legal system and history and culture, many terms and norms in Chinese law do not exist in English; that is to say, there is no equivalence between the two.

In the translation of legal terms, we should first of all pay attention to the differences between English and Chinese cultural backgrounds and ways of thinking; secondly, according to these differences, we should be consistent with our legal habits and usage and try to translate into authentic legal terms. In addition, we should translate the terms from facts based on our accurate understanding of the original meaning of the legal terms through understanding their specific context.

In conclusion, the translation of legal terms is a kind of intercultural communication within the framework of the legal system, and it has its own characteristics and principles. The translators should be guided by functional equivalence theory, have an in-depth understanding of English and Chinese legal language and the legal system of both countries, adopt appropriate translation strategies and methods according to the needs of legal and cultural exchange, so as to "constitute a positive and limited framework for innovation which is confined to legal, linguistic, cultural and other factors" (Du, 2004).

References

Bao, K. (2011). On the unequivalence of English and Chinese legal terms and their translation strategies. *Chinese Science and Technology Translators Journal, 4*, 32–34.

Chen, Z. (2000). *Laws translation.* China Legal Publishing House.

Dong, X. (2011). *Translation of legal texts.* University of International Business and Economics Press.

Du, J. (2004). *Forensic linguistics.* Shanghai Foreign Language Education Press.

Garner, B. A. (2004). *Black's law dictionary* (8th ed.). Thomson West Group.

Li, K., & Zhang, X. (2006). *Legal texts and legal translation.* China Translation and Publishing Corporation.

Liang, S. (2014). A study of textual translation and the subjectivity of translators from the perspective of intertextuality. *Research, 9*, 120–124.

Liu, R. (2010). On the accuracy of legal terminology translation. *Foreign Language Research, 4*, 125–127.

Sarcevic, S. (1997). *New approaches to legal translation.* Kluwer Law International.

Tan, F., & Xiang, H. (2012). Cross-cultural translation of legal English terms from functional equivalence theory perspective. *Contemporary Foreign Languages Studies, 10*, 52–55.

Xiao, Y. (2001). The characteristics, etymology and translation of English and Chinese legal terms. *Chinese Translators Journal, 3*, 44–47.

Xiong, D. (2010). "Prometheus" in legal translation in late Qing Dynasty and its special contribution. *Foreign Language Education, 5*, 94–97.

Chapter 8
Possible Strategies for Modern Laws and Regulations Translation

8.1 Introduction

As the significance of laws and regulations translation has changed with the times from the passive to active part, legal translation itself is now not only representing the will of the country but also undertaking the mission of enhancing its cultural soft power and building a rule of law country image. From the 1980s, some foreign scholars, in particular, the American professional professors of studying China's laws, not only translated China's civil law but also diverted their attention to Chinese traditional legal culture. Gradual improvement in China's legal system attracted more attention from the world (Wang, 2018). In other words, western countries also joined in the translation of China's laws and regulations. As the dominant force leading the whole work of translation, based on its pivotal significance, we have to heighten our self-consciousness of subjectivity in securing the norms of translation as much as possible. Confronted with the violation of norms in current legal translation, the top priority for us is, under the guidance of norm theory, to re-examine the existing problems and try to give solutions in a systematic and complete manner, both from the macro and micro level, and comprehensively taking the whole process of translation into account within the social and cultural system.

8.2 Strengthening the Project Management of Laws and Regulations Translation

Traditional translation with simple form, out of cultural communication and academic publishing etc., was usually finished by individuals, and the quality of translation solely depended on translator's capability and attainment. With the further development of economic globalization, there is a swiftly soaring tendency of translation service. In a sense, the so-called translation industry is emerging, serving more diversified industries. A variety of factors, including the increasing workload of

X. Dong and Y. Zhang, *Chinese Legal Translation and Language Planning in the New Era*, https://doi.org/10.1007/978-981-19-8448-8_8

translation, limited time schedule, strict client requirement, and advanced translation technology, have led to the growing complication of translation work. Translation project management, which is of artistic, scientific and professional integration, has become a critical link in the whole process of translation precisely because it involves communication and interaction in multi facets (Wang & Wang, 2012).

Project is a temporary work for creating distinctive products, service or achievements. Temporariness is characterized by, specifically, the definite starting and terminating points. The work itself is temporary but the results are expected to generate lasting impact (Project Management Institute, 2013). Laws and regulations translation is also a temporary work, catering to the characteristics of a project, with time limitation. Due to the timeliness, some English versions of laws and regulations are always released simultaneously with their Chinese versions, while others lagging behind within a certain time period which lasts not too long. Project management is the process of application of knowledge, skills, tools and technology to project activity to meet its requirement. According to the logic relation, the whole process of project management can be classified into five stages, namely, project initiating, project planning, project executing, project controlling, and project closing. As a matter of fact, the executing and controlling phases are always intertwined and overlapped. Consequently, translation project management can generally be divided into four stages, that is, project initiating, project planning, project executing, and project closing. And the key factors in translation project management mainly include translation communication management, quality management, language assets management, and financial management.

As for the laws and regulations translation, normally funded by the governments, it is slightly different from the work done by translation corporations seeking profits. The four stages can by and large explained as follows: the phase of project initiating mainly contains the assessment of the project and selection of translators; the phase of project planning primarily contains the formulation of the time schedule, the distribution of workload, and the unification of the English expressions of key terminology; the phase of project executing chiefly contains keeping track of the quality of translation by sampling inspection; and the phase of project closing largely contains the reviewing and proofreading of the translated texts. For those who started late in translating local regulations and rules, project management is more of a mode of thinking which make the whole translation normalized. Through procedural management, the translation was brought under control and supervision.

In addition, translation communication management also implies to us that there is both horizontal and vertical communication between departments of different levels. With regard to the vertical communication, in order to avoid the discrepancy of English translation of legal terminology between upper-level legislation and lower-level legislation, there should be more communication among the legislative affairs offices of the country level and local level. For instance, the much-experienced experts of laws translation of national level can be regularly invited to give guidance on the local regulations and rules translation by symposium or training classes. The standardization work done by the country level should also be better publicized to the local level by smooth communication.

With regard to the horizontal communication, especially referring to the local level, it involves wider scope including not only translators and translators, and translators and legislators within one translation group of a certain region, but also the communication between different regions. By project management, establishing communication mechanism is precisely the focal point for translators to secure the consistency of terms and expressions. Legal translation is not a simple process of information decoding, but an act of communication within the mechanism of the law (Sarcevic, 1997). Communication between translators and legislators is increasingly important because nowadays legislation is becoming a more and more professional work. Complicated is the connotation and intention of the legislation texts with some necessary judicial interpretation sometimes. And the translation of local regulations and rules also are under the influence of legislation intention itself, upper-level legislation, and official translation tradition (Li & Dong, 2015). During translation, the translators, being not members of the legislators, or without professional knowledge of laws, might fail to get the real intention and meaning of many regulations and rules. Therefore, receiving support from the legislation department seems to be a must. Finally, some local governments started the translation work of local regulations and rules earlier and others relatively late. The communication between regions should also be strengthened so that the late one can also learn from the early one to improve the wider communication and secure the consistency of translation between different regions.

All in all, to establish the regular communication, exchange and coordination mechanism among departments is sure to greatly improve the development of China's translation cause (Li, 2017). The project management of legal translation demands a comprehensive and complete way of thinking, considering from both the horizontal and vertical angle and from the whole process of translation, to establish a systematic mechanism to strengthen the communication norm and quality norm of the translation.

8.3 Reinforcing Cultivation of Interdisciplinary Legal Translation Talents

As Xi Jinping pointed out, to participate in global governance, we need a host of professional talents who are not only familiar with the guidelines and policies of our Party and country but also are of global horizon, and can skillfully use foreign languages, get to know the international rules and have a good command of international negotiation. Team of talents in global governance should be strengthened to break through the bottleneck and make talents preparation, offering talents support for China's participation in global governance (Chen, 2017).

To establish the norms of legal translation, interdisciplinary legal translation talents cultivation is precisely the bottleneck that we should break through. Cultivation of talents is a systematic project, involving a series of prominent problems including teaching aims, faculty of legal translation, curriculum arrangement, teaching schedule, translation practice and cultivation system etc. (Zhang, 2018). The top priority should be given to the training and cultivation of interdisciplinary faculty of legal translation. Dual strategies can be adopted including "bringing in" and "going out" (Dong, 2017). The former refers to recruiting qualified teachers from home and abroad while the later cultivating and training within the universities by integration of faculty from both school of foreign languages and cultures and school of laws, promoting the transition from the language-oriented teachers to the law subject oriented ones. With qualified faculty, a series of problems including the proper teaching aims, optimized curriculum system, improved teaching methods and adequate translation practice can also be gradually resolved in a comprehensive manner.

In addition, interdisciplinary talents can also be cultivated through think tank. Since the convening of the 18th CPC National Congress, there has been a rapid development of new type of think tank construction. In 2014, Ministry of Education of People's Republic of China released a *Notice of Promoting Plan of Construction of New Type of Universities' Think Tanks with Chinese Characteristics*, noting that universities' think tanks should function as means of strategic research, policy suggestion, talents cultivation, public opinion guidance and public diplomacy and interdisciplinary think tank talents should be cultivated as the talent support and guarantee.

Since the socialism with Chinese characteristics has entered into the new era, laws and regulations translation is of critical significance, not only contributing Chinese wisdom to the global governance but also enhancing China's cultural soft power. Talents cultivation also appeals to new modes and methods. Think tank research is characterized by the integration and combination of multi disciplines and researchers (Wang, 2017). Through assembling the elites from different subjects and fields, think tank is conducting research oriented to the requirement of national strategy. One of the noticeable characters of the top-level think tank in universities abroad is to merge into the talent cultivation system of their subordinate colleges or schools. For instance, advanced researchers in Hoover Institution of Stanford University mostly undertake the responsibility of cultivating students and curriculum teaching. The institute also offers practice posts for students in the project research.

Certainly, this is a good experience for us to draw from. Universities in China can establish think tank oriented in *China's Moderation of Rule of Law and its External Publicity* from the whole universities level by the combination of faculty from the school of foreign languages and cultures, school of laws and school of communication etc., even by bringing in the elite experts from governments and renowned universities from the world. Through project research, regional cooperation, international communication and academic exchange, teams of faculty can widen its serving fields and develop the external talents cultivation system, including the writing of textbooks, curriculum schedule and practice base development etc. By combining researchers from different disciplines, think tank is the new and innovative pathway to cultivate interdisciplinary talents.

8.4 Highlighting Continuous Standardization Work

The work of standardization is of vital significance to secure the quality of translation, which is not only an activity of knowledge innovation but also the publicity of it, worthy of being extremely highlighted. In reviewing and approving the terms, as practice tells us, individual capability is the basis, collective wisdom is the key point, and way of operation is the guarantee (Li, 2012). As a systematic work, we should consider it in a comprehensive and scientific way with a set of complete mechanism.

Since the separation of practice and research still exists, we cannot expect that the standardization work will be done just by the self-consciousness of the translators. In effect, it is also hard to accomplish without the concerted efforts. Standardization work itself is so complicated that there must be concerning departments, especially the department of translation practice, for instance, Legislative Affairs Office of the State Council of the People's Republic of China, actively leading the tasks with the adequate financial support, sound mechanism construction and qualified teams of personnel etc.…

Standardization should be equipped with a team of professional talents who specialize in doing this job. In addition to a team of translators, it is also a must for organizing a professional team of standardization, including experienced experts of jurisprudence, linguistics, Chinese language and foreign languages, in light of the significance of laws and regulations translation. Independent from translation itself, by regularly standardizing the laws and regulations translation, the team and its achievements gradually become the authoritative guidance for whole country's laws and regulations translation.

Standardization should follow the principle of being systematic. On the one hand, terms in laws and regulations of the country level as well as regulations and rules of the local level should be consistent, which needs the organization to follow the communication norm from top to bottom, that is, strengthening the coordination from upper-level legislation to lower-level legislation and the cooperation and communication from regions to regions. On the other hand, it implies that both the terms translation in legislative texts and other related legal texts, such as, terms in administrative enforcement of law of police, frontier guard, and customs, should be standardized in a complete way (Qu, 2012), or rather, terms used in different departments involving translation should also be standardized at the same time. The standardization in laws and regulations translation is solely one part of the whole legal translation.

Standardization should be technicalization with the established technical norms. As the development of language service industry, there is a growing emergence of Computer-aided Translation. New software is gradually applied in translation, which can substantially improve translators' productivity and optimize the translation process (Xu et al., 2007). By the application of CAT, a lot of work can be done conveniently, such as, establishing Chinese-English parallel corpus which will facilitate the consulting and retrieving of words and expressions and realizing better management of the language assets. Most computer-aided translation tools, such as, SDL Trados, Deja vu X, MemoQ, OmegaT etc., are equipped with basic function of management. The common commercial management system includes Across Language Server, Beetext Flow, GlobalLink GMS, Kilgray MemoQ, Language Networks Espresso, MultiTrans Prism, Plunet Business Manager, Project-open, SDL Trados Synergy, SDL WorldServer, and Translation Office 3000 etc. and some companies even develop their own terminology extraction tools, such as, SDL MultiTerm Exract, acrolinx IQ Terminology Manager, Across crossTerm, AnyLexic, BeeText Term, Heartsome Dictinary Editor, and LogiTerm etc. (Cui & Luo, 2016). By language assets, it refers to the language resources produced in translation. After many years of laws and regulations translation, a lot of results or products have been accomplished which are also called language assets. The language assets are mainly comprised of terminology and translation memory. Actually, both help to establish the language database, which can definitely improve translation working efficiency, knowledge share and faster pace of problems solving in the terminology management system.

Standardization should be regular and routine. Laws and regulations translation is an everlasting activity because the new laws and regulations always emerge with the pace of the times and local regulations and rules translation also bears its distinctive characteristics. As the guarantee and guidance of translation quality, standardization work should also be continuous. However, the connotation of standardization should not be limited to compilation of dictionary and establishment of database, because repetitive compilation of dictionary and construction of database of low level might in part facilitate translation but fail to secure the standardization and unification of translation. It is still necessary for the re-standardization of even the already standardized English translation of terms, which is a process of striving for perfection.

At last, standardization work should strengthen its publicity. There do still exist such problems as the scarce use of previously mentioned handbook compiled for terms and sentences translation. A variety of reasons contribute to this, such as the inconvenient use of the handbook to look up words and expressions, but the most important is the lack of publicity. Standardization results itself should become the quality norm that the translators will strictly observe. Therefore, special publishing and distribution channel should be established for the latest standardization achievements to make sure that translators engaging in legal translation will get to know it and consciously apply it.

8.5 Advancing Theoretical Research and Its Application

As Xi Jinping pointed out in his report at 19th CPC National Congress, we will work faster to develop philosophy and social sciences with Chinese characteristics. Nowadays, strong philosophy and social sciences, with academic research as the core, are the basis for us to establish external discourse system, which can help us to gain international power of discourse. Discourse systems of western countries are powerful precisely because they have solid theoretical research and innovative concepts which make western theories win international popularity.

As one indispensable part of philosophy and social sciences, both legal translation practice and its theoretical research bear the distinctive significance, not only helping us to enhance our cultural soft power, but also helping us to gain the international power of discourse. It is known to us all that translation thoughts can drive action and translation theory can propel practice.At its core, the theory is also beneficial to discerning the truth from false, distinguishing the right from wrong and improving our judgment (Liu, 2019).

Theoretical research is the spring of the innovation of concepts, terms and categories. The theory of legal translation develops by drawing nourishment from other disciplines. However, current academic research mainly involves the system-functional linguistics, and the translator's subjectivity and relevance theory (Zhang & He, 2012). Dominated by western theories in translation research, it is urgent for us to build our own system of translation theory with Chinese values. Since we have actively devoted to laws and regulations translation, China's translation theory research should be rooted in China's practice. That is not to say that we should give up all the western theories. On the contrary, on the basis of borrowing ideas from them, we will also add some Chinese elements. China has a long history of translation theory, leaving us a large number of achievements in translation research. What should be done is to, following the principle of cultural confidence and by learning from western theories, inherit, summarize, innovate and develop our own translation theory with distinctive Chinese style, establishing the translation theory system and publicizing it to the world (Luo, 1983).

Generally speaking, translation research is divided into three hierarchies, that is, research on methods, strategies and thoughts. Research on methods is normally the direct experience gained from the translation practice. Research on strategies is the reflection on the problems and the discovery and recognition of the natural law of translation. Research on thoughts is of holistic insights into the essence of translation. In other words, people's recognition of translation is sure to evolve from the micro level to macro level. Macro level research, from the holistic perspective, bears the significance of relative guidance and overall planning, while micro research is full of much translation experience and many techniques. For the translators, both are all indispensable part of theoretical research. Usually, the micro level research is so close to the translation practice involving many specific problems that it attracts many scholars to devote to it. That explains why more research at present remains on the macro or micro level, and there is still much room for the research into legal translation from the macro level (Shan & Fan, 2018), to make legal translation theoretical research more systematic.

In addition, communication should also be strengthened between the departments of theory research and translation practice. Theoretical work is not done for the sake of itself but also for publicizing new thoughts and new knowledge. The new standardization results of legal translation by researchers should be released to the professional translators through much publicity, training classes and symposiums etc. A series of measures should be taken to improve the application of latest research achievements, such as, to establish the cooperation organization between translation practice and research departments, build a specialist team of translation practice and research, actively apply the results of translation research to guiding regulations and rules translation practice, and adjust the translation research aims according to the translation practice (Du et al., 2004).

8.6 Conclusion

The significance of translation changes with the times. In the historical development of translation, it has largely evolved into three stages, namely, the first phase dominated by translating religion and classics, the second phase dominated by translating literary masterpieces and classics of social sciences, and the third phase of translating practical materials and texts, also called the professionalized phase, specifically speaking, the translation of commercial documents and papers of national governments and international organizations (Xie, 2015). Correspondingly, the significance of translation has altered from original pure cultural communication into nowadays the wider category and translation is increasingly becoming a crucial approach for serving the national development and participation in the global governance (Zhu, 2019). The significance of translation has been uplifted to a certain place in China. At the same time, the vital significance also requires us to consider and study translation from the perspective of the language-centered to cross disciplines paradigm (Wang, 2015), rather than being limited to the level of both languages.

In this day and age, enhancing China's cultural soft power, a most important premise for Chinese nation's great rejuvenation, is not only a key strategic point in our cultural development but also an indispensable part of our strategic thoughts of developing a harmonious world. The soft power is the force represented in a nation's culture and ideology. Undoubtedly, as a communication bridge and method, translation is increasingly becoming an essential part of cultural soft power in China. Needless to say, the sound and healthy development of translation industry is sure to secure the quality of translation and contribute to developing China's image in the world.

Influenced by both internal and external factors, legal translation is definitely a norm-governed activity. Currently, as in its initial stage of development with larger demand of translation work, there is inevitable violation of norms in legal translation practice. Certainly, translation norms grow increasingly mature as translation industry develops. However, it doesn't mean that we just wait and cannot do anything at all. On the contrary, it is necessary for us to actively consider legal translation in a comprehensive and systematic way under the guidance of norm theory. Following the preliminary norms, preparation and selection of appropriate translators requires us to reinforce the cultivation of interdisciplinary legal translation talents. In accordance with the operational norms, we should strengthen the project management of laws and regulations translation, improving the accountability norm, relation norm and communication norm. At the same time, standardization of legal translation should go along with the practice, which is a continuous activity and under the guidance with advanced theoretical research. Considering form the post translation phase, management of language assents and theoretical research with Chinese style are also sure to further guarantee the sound development of relation norm.

All in all, China is now actively engaging in legal translation because it is now shouldering more responsibilities than ever before in the world. The world order is also gradually coordinated by international rules and norms. Laws and regulations are one of the latest achievements gained in China's modernization of rule of law. Only through translation can they really contribute Chinese wisdom to the global governance. Active participation in developing norms of translation can also stir its development to positive direction. This is not only conducive to the whole legal translation industry but also to enhancing China's cultural soft power and facilitating its participation in global governance.

References

Chen, X. (2017). *General Secretary Xi Jinping's thoughts on global governance.* Retrieved August 17, 2017, from http://theory.people.com.cn/n1/2017/0817/c83859-29476848.html

Cui, Q., & Luo, H. (2016). *Project management for translation and localization.* Foreign Languages Press.

Dong, X. (2017, October 22). On the importance of interdisciplinary foreign languages talent cultivation under the Belt and Road Initiative. *Guangming Daily.*

Du, J., Zhang, F., & Yuan, L. (2004). Problems of English translation of China's laws and regulations and their solution. *Chinese Translators Journal, 3*, 74–78.

Li, J. (2012). Standardizing terms and prospering ethnic culture. *Journal of Minzu University of China (Philosophy and Social Sciences Edition), 3*, 89–93.

Li, J., & Dong, X. (2015). The standardization of translation of local rules and regulations and its countermeasures—A research based on translation practice for rules and regulations in Jiangsu Province. *Southeast Academic Research, 5*, 225–233. https://doi.org/10.13658/j.cnki.sar.2015.05.032

Li, X. (2017). Improve political terms translation to serve China's external publicity. *Foreign Languages Research, 2*, 81–85.

Liu, M. (2019). *Translation thinking in China and in the West.* China Translation & Publishing House.

Luo, X. (1983). China's own system of translation theory (continuation). *Chinese Translators Journal, 8*, 8–12.

Project Management Institute. (2013). *A guide to the project management body of knowledge (PMBOK guide)* (5th ed.). Publishing House of Electronics Industry.

Qu, W. (2012). Problems of China's legal terminology translation and its reason reflection—A discussion on the standardization of legal terminology. *Chinese Translators Journal, 6*, 68–75.

Sarcevic, S. (1997). *New approaches to legal translation.* Kluwer Law International.

Shan, Y., & Fan, W. (2018). A knowledge mapping analysis of legal translation studies in China (1992–2016)—Based on the 702 research documents of CNKI. *Contemporary Foreign Languages Studies, 4*, 85–93.

Wang, H. (2017). *Theoretical paradigm and practical innovation of construction of universities' think tanks.* World Affairs Press.

Wang, H. (2018). The output track of translating Chinese legal literature and its enlightenment. *Political Science and Law, 11,* 117–126. https://doi.org/10.15984/j.cnki.1005-9512.2018.11.010

Wang, H., & Wang, H. (2012). *A practical guide to translation project management.* China Publishing & Media Holdings Co., Ltd. & China Translation Corporation.

Wang, N. (2015). New definition of translation from the perspective of cross disciplines and visual culture. *Chinese Translators Journal, 3,* 13–16.

Xie, T. (2015). New orientation and definition of translation. *Chinese Translators Journal, 3,* 14–15.

Xu, B., Guo, H., & Guo, X. (2007). Applications of computer-aided translation: An overview. *Shandong Foreign Language Teaching, 4,* 77–80.

Zhang, F. (2018). On legal translation teaching and talents cultivation under the Belt and Road Initiative. *Chinese Translators Journal, 2,* 31–35.

Zhang, T., & He, Z. (2012). Research progress on law translation in China. *Hebei Law Science, 2,* 152–157. https://doi.org/10.16494/j.cnki.1002-3933.2012.02.008

Zhu, Y. (2019). New era, new discourse and new thinking of external publicity. *Chinese Translators Journal, 1,* 117–122.

Chapter 9
Legal Language Planning in the New Era

9.1 Introduction

In the field of law, language problems are essential. As the carrier and tool of legislative intent and legislative objective, language plays a pivotal role in legislative activities. As the formation and improvement of socialist legal system has been realized, the language problems and language planning in China's field of law is becoming the focus of the sociolinguistics study. In the last decade, legal language problems are in the ascendant in academic circle and related discussion never cease to happen (Dong, 2004, 2006, 2007, 2013; Liu, 2009; Pan, 2007; Song & Chen, 2009; Wang, 2010; Zou, 2012; Zhang, 2013), and these discussions from macroscopic to microcosmic, all concern various language problems in the field of law, ranging from language status planning, corpus planning, acquisition planning to spreading planning, largely reflecting the diversity and urgency of problems in this area and the necessity of conducting corresponding systematic study on language planning.

Language has been placed in indispensable position since ages ago. The western saying "the law is simply a matter of linguistics." at some degree, reflects the maturity of study of language planning in other countries and it is becoming more advanced in depth and width of study. On the contrary, study on language planning in the field of law in China has not been systematized and the current study has been limited on research focus, insensitive to problems and lacking in systematicness. Study on language planning is a new crucial task in China. Li (2013) pointed out in his discourse on domain language situation that law plays a vital role in national language situation management. Today, Four Chinese Jurisdictions would remain in Chinese mainland, Hong Kong, Macao and Taiwan for a long time. The in-depth investigation and study on the state, attitude, ability, status, belief and communication of language will help eliminate in Four Chinese Jurisdictions the disagreement, misunderstanding and obstacles among legislation, administrative enforcement and justice system, improving the unification and standardization of law and the development of economy in four areas across the straits. In this spirit, this paper will

X. Dong and Y. Zhang, *Chinese Legal Translation and Language Planning in the New Era*, https://doi.org/10.1007/978-981-19-8448-8_9

present the commentary in brief on study on legal language planning and investigate language problems in the field of law in China and the method of language planning study, hoping to further the conduction of in-depth study on language planning in the field of law in China.

9.2 An Overview of Study on Legal Language Planning

Language planning in the field of law is an interdisciplinary (at least concerns linguistics, jurisprudence, literature, communication, pedagogy and sociology) and problem-oriented practical issue and it is new in areas including language competition and communication of cultural soft power. Jurists in early ancient Roman Empire placed much importance on the perfection and usage of legal language when they gave assistance in the legislation of Roman Empire, compilation of legal literature and solution to legal problems. In Europe, after the publishment of an early writing on legal language *On Legislative Expression* by George Coode, treatises on similar issues are not large in number in the middle and late half of nineteenth century and the first half of twentieth century. It is when forensic linguistics is listed as an independent discipline in Europe and the U.S. that fruitful and insightful study on legal language, which is deemed as a crucial area, has been conducted, for instance, *Legislative Drafting* by Diekerson in 1981; *The Language of the Law* by Mellinkoff in 1963; *Legal Writing Style* by Weihofen in 1979, etc. After late 1970s, with the deep development of immigration and civil rights, ethnic relationships and ethnic issues related to language are catching increasing attention and language legislation and language policy has become the significant decision of multiracial countries around the current world, making language legislation reform and study on language policy new focuses for sociolinguistics. According to Israeli scholar Spolsky's statistics (2011), throughout the world, constitution in about 125 countries involves certain language policy; about 100 countries designate one or more languages as their official language or national language, which all are endowed with privilege of use; more than a half of the countries designate one official language or national language (or rather, 78 countries).

In general, foreign study on language planning in the field of law has a great variety of perspectives and has already formed a multilevel theoretic and practical research system concerning individual researcher, academic school, universities, scientific research institution and national think tank. As Haugen (1968), an America born Norwegian linguist, stated in 1968, that language planning can be classified as status planning and corpus planning. In 1989 Cooper added acquisition planning as another type. Based on these three types of language planning, in consideration of the characteristics of fusion of language, culture and exchange in the field of law, spreading planning can possibly be added as another type of language planning, which makes four practicable types of language planning with regard to the overall development of legal language and translation in total.

1. Study on Status Planning of Legal Language

Status planning, in its essence, is legislation of language to confirm the status and value of language and allocate the usage, function and occasions applicable of language. The focus of status planning in the field of law is the choice of national official language (especially the choice of legislative language and its force), the choice of judicial language and the protection and use of language right of the minority.

Wright (2012) believes that the legal identification and popularization of national language provide the society with a social community which is necessary for the operation of a nation state and serve as an important factor during the progress of building national identity. *National Language Policy*, promulgated in 1987 by the Department of Education of Australian government, is the nation's first official language policy that clearly identified English as the national and official language of Australia; *Language and Language Right Policy of Australia*, passed by the Australian parliament in 1991, marks that Australia began to attach more importance to preserve and develop its aboriginal language while promoting English nationwide. In Edington (1994)'s view, Australia's language policy is a model for countries with similar cultural and historical background. In *Official Languages Act*, passed by the Canadian Parliament in 1969, English and French are at the same time established as Canada's official legislative language with equal validity. This is reaffirmed in *Constitution of Canada* and the *Canadian Charter of Rights and Freedoms* in 1982, which also stipulated that Indians and other ethnic minority shall have the right to learn their own language. In 1988, world's first *Multiculturalism Act* was passed by the Canadian Parliament. The Canadian Multiculturalism Act further strengthened two official languages' position and at the same time clearly put forward that the use of other languages should be protected and enhanced. Fishman (1966), after summarizing the progress of America's "de-ethnization" and "English-only movement", holds the idea that "the self-sustaining progress of immigrants relating to their own languages and cultures permeate the entire history of the United State". America changed language assimilation legislation in 1968 by introducing the *Bilingual Education Act* that was aimed at Hispanic immigrants. US's former president George Bush signed the *Native American Language Act* which confirmed with legislation Native American language's special status and its special contribution to American national tradition and culture. Karetu (1997) gives an account of the course during which Maori dedicated to protecting and developing the right to use Māori language for a long time. Before the *Māori Language Act* which marked that Māori language became one of New Zealand's official languages and enjoy the same validity as English was drafted in 1974, English had been New Zealand's only official language and only teaching language in Maori schools according to government's law.

As the government of a multi-ethnic, multi-language and multi-culture country, the Chinese Government has always been paying attention to the important position of language planning in safeguarding national unity, promote ethnic solidarity and Socialist Modernization. *The Law of the National Commonly-Used Language and Scrip of the People's Republic of China* is the first specific law about language and script of China, which stipulates that existing languages and scripts in China are all equal with mandarin and standard Chinese characters as the country's commonly-used language and script. In ethnic minority autonomous area and areas inhabited by the minority nationalities, national commonly-used language and script and the minority languages and scripts should be used simultaneously.

In conclusion, across the world, language status planning of multi-ethnic countries tends to show different features concerning language legislation and culture in different countries or areas, which is determined by different societies, economies, politics, ideologies, faiths and cultures. But with the advancement of societies and development of times, Linguistic Rights as a significant measurement of every group's rights of life and rights of ethnic equality, have become a pivotal part in every country's language policy. A study from Spolsky (2011), an Israeli scholar, shows that research method of linguistic rights developed quickly during the second half of the twentieth century all around the world, especially Western Europe and the United States. It is worth thinking about our scholars, especially linguistic scholars, live in a multi-ethnic and multi-language country, yet few of them give some thought and research to linguistic rights from the multi-dimensional perspective. Only several law learners showed alertness and reflection over this question (Xiao, 2010, 2012; Guo, 2011; Weng, 2011).

2. Study on Corpus Planning of Legal Language

Corpus planning refers to the modification of language itself, with the purpose of normalizing and completing the language of the law, which as a result will perform functions given by status planning better. Linguistic planning consists of lexicography, explanation of grammar, revision of terms as well as the completion and normalization of the writing system. Wright (2012), a British linguist, regards "normalization, standardization, and regularization" as the second point of corpus planning of language at the nation level, aiming at making law which is carried by language, in every field of every country, causes the least possible misunderstanding and produces the highest efficiency.

Brierly (1942) believes that the main work of legislative drafters is "to express legal content in a language that is clearer and more appropriate than the existing legal texts." The plain English movement in English-speaking countries during 1920s, through language modifications including reducing the use of legal terminology, avoiding complex grammatical structure, using active voice, short sentences and personal Pronoun, preferring affirmative expressions, as well as avoiding multi-negation and specific words, legal language was simplified, which helps parties understand legal language and promotes the normalization of English-speaking countries' legal language. Weihofen (1979), an expert of legal language points out that "a lawyer cannot do his work before he understands legal terms and simplified legal language." According to a study from Zhou (2009) shows that professional corpus planning of language in western countries' field of law were already countless before the Second World War.

During the formation of China's socialist legal system, people are becoming increasingly certain that language standardization is in line with the rule of law while language non-standardization is contrary to the rule of law which is a reflection of unsound law-ruling system. For more than 30 years, domestic scholars have made great progress in the study of corpus planning of legal language. They focus on two aspects: the first one is to actively tackle the urgently problems to be solved, such as the language standardization of the current "Constitution" studied by distinguished linguists and constitutional scholars like Jianming Lu and Renbo Wang, the language standardization of the current "Criminal Law" studied by the fifteenth research of National Language Committee hosted by Xie Ying, and the language standardization of the *Property Law (Draft)* passed in 2005 studied jointly by linguist professor Wang Jie and civil jurist professor Xu Guodong; the second is that interdisciplinary, multi-view and globalization has become a trend, such as Song (2006), Liao (2008), Dong (2013), etc.

The studies home and abroad have indicated that the corpus standardization of legal language is a vitally important and integral part of the national legal construction. As forensic linguistic professor Liao (2008) noted, "Legal language civilization is a vitally important and integral part of law civilization; in order to standardize human's behavior effectively, law should be standardized for its language first; The era of legal construction calls for study of standardization of legal language…".

3. Study on Acquisition Planning of Legal Language

The study of acquisition planning of legal language is the study of legal language itself rather than that of Mandarin or official language in which the law enacted. As a language for special purpose, legal language is other than common language for it has particularity. Mellinkoff (1963) defined it in his book, *the Language of the Law*, "the language attorneys often use in general judicial activities in countries whose official language is English." However, it is a very narrow definition for excluding the language of legislator, judge and law-executor. Take Legal English for example, it is known as legal language or language of the law in English country which refers to the language or part of the language in which law subject and litigation or non-litigation legal affairs are expressed. As a branch of English for specific purposes (ESP), legal language has characteristics like that of ESP. Huchtson et al. (2002), a British scholar, said: realizing the designated goal by using the language is the aim rather than the language itself. The acquisition planning of legal language aims to serving the professional lines of work with language (or English). Therefore, courses are instituted to suit specific requirements of learners, and the learning is focused on the language (grammar, vocabulary, register), text and genre adapted to the profession.

As for the language education program in China, some colleges have set up the Legal English courses since the end of 1970s to the beginning of 1980s. In recent years, an increasing number of local colleges have also set up the Legal English courses as a direction of ESP, Guangdong University of Foreign Studies, Zhongnan University of Economics and Law, Nanjing Normal University, for example. There have been more than 20 kinds of legal English textbooks which can be divided into three categories: the first is copies of foreign legal books; the second is bilingual textbooks written by Chinese scholars like Zhu (2007), Yuan (2012), etc.; the third which is also the most is Anglo-American legal English textbooks written by Chinese scholars, such as Sha (1997), Dong (1997), Du (2008), Dong (2009, 2011a, 2011b), etc. Scientific papers gradually turn their research perspectives to macroscopic problems like teaching ideas, aim and the complex talents development of legal English from microcosmic problems like language feature, vocabulary and grammar of legal English. It is worth mentioning that study of legal Chinese planning in China is not as sufficient as that of legal English planning. There is generally not so many achievements except those of Liu (2003), Pan (2004), Ning (2007) and others, which may has some relationship to the attention to Chinese university system and English learning.

4. Study on Spreading Planning of Legal Language

In the field of law, the spread of language is that law of nation (including tribe) A is learned by nation (including tribe) B through the language of the former to spread the legal law of nation A (also called language possessive) to nation B (also called language receiver). Translation is an important way to spread language. For the involved areas, the spread of legal language through translation can be generally divided into two categories: one is domestic spread which means translation of legal language among different nationalities within a country, for example, to translate "Constitution of the People's Republic of China" Chinese version into Uygur version, Mongolian version, etc.; another is international spread which means to translate legal language of a country into that of another, such as translating the Chinese version of the *Constitution of the People's Republic of China* into English version or the English version of the *Constitution of the United States of America* into Chinese version.

The fundamental motive of language spread lies in its value. Only valuable language can be learned and used by other nationalities or countries and so is legal language. Language is a tool for communication (Knapp et al., 2009; Widdowson, 2003) and identity basis (Gumperz, 1982; Holmes et al., 2003). Language spread has the function of assimilating different nations. Providing with multilingual legal texts is the general rule of countries, areas or international organizations those enforce bilingual or multilingual legislation like Canada, Hong Kong, European Union, etc. The *New Approach to Legal Translation* by Croatian professor Susan Šarčević has a significant impact on Chinese legal translation, one chapter of it talking specifically about unification and standardization of legal communication (or legal translation).

In the recent years, the National People's Congress, the Legal Affairs Office of the State Council and the Legal Affairs Office of all the provinces build professional teams to do law, regulations and rules translation. The research on the problems and solutions of the legal translation spreading is on the rise. Scholars like Du et al. (2004), Dong (2011a, 2011b) and Qu (2012) all point out the importance of the standardized research on legal translation spreading. Compared with foreign countries, the domestic research of the legal translation faces a situation where the scholars in law, linguistics and translation carry out separated, isolated, repeated research which leads to nowhere. In particular, there is a serious blank on the spreading research of the domestic legal translation, for instance, very few of the scholars study the spreading of converting the mandarin legal text to other languages spoken by the ethnic minorities in China, and nearly no related paper can be found in the China academic periodical net.

9.3 Research Framework Construction of Legal Language Planning

Li (2013) argued that field language planning enjoys an important position in the national language life management which on the one hand connects with the national language policy, on the other hand involves into the language life of the corporation and public institution that belongs to the end chain of all walks of life. The basic content of the field language planning is consisted of two parts: the first is to support the national language policy, the second is to build the language standardization related to the work quality, the third is to resolve the field language problems. Therefore, I think in order to systematically carry out the language planning research in the field of Chinese law, we could sort out the main-body layer as well as the specific language problem field of the language planning concerning field of Chinese law from macro, medium and micro levels according to the related theories of language planning and language policies and the specific characteristics of the language problems in the field of law. The following is a simple research graph.

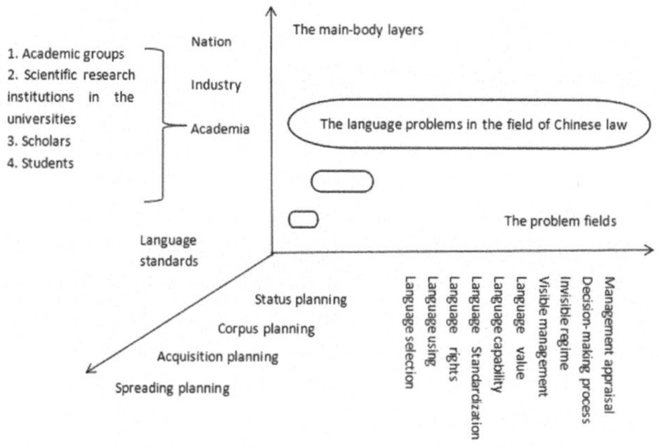

1. The Main-Body Layer in the Field of Law in China

The task of the traditional language planning is to do intervention, management and make related plans about the language life of which the main planner are the nation and the government. While the modern language planning thinks that language planning and language policies are multilayer planning activities of multi-participation analyzed from the whole process of formulating, implementing, evaluating and adjusting, especially the language planning within the field (Ricento & Hornberger, 1996). Li (2013) holds the view that the basic operation mechanism of the field language planning should be governed by the competent department, guided by the national functional department and academically supported by the specialist team. In the field of law, language planning at least involves the following different main-body layers from macro to micro aspect.

(1) The National Layer

The legislative institution is responsible for the language legislation, making sure the position and value of different languages, distributing the function of the language and regulating the language using occasion. The functional department (the administrative institution and the judicial organ) provide joint guidance for the language planning in the field of law and manage the condition of the language life concerning the field of law within the scope of functions and powers as prescribed by the law, that's to say to have an in-depth understanding of the language life condition in the field of law, adjust the national language policies in time within the law framework so as to conform to the language life reality in the field of law, set out the detailed rules in the field of law according to the national language policies and make them to be carried out more effectively.

(2) The Industrial Layer

Generally speaking, the language life of the competent department of the industry and the industry association possesses reasonability theoretically and feasibility operationally (Li, 2013). At present, one of the main problems of the language life within the field of law is that the officer leaders of the judicial organ and related associations are lack of language awareness and the common knowledge of linguistics. They know little about the relationship between the law language and the society as well as the present condition of the language life in the field of law. Particularly in the globalized, informationized, internationalized and multi-cultural era, we should figure out the language talents needed in the field of law, the way to rape the "dividend" in the field of law by taking the advantage of languages and letters, and the way to handle the relationship between the languages in the field of law to ease or even avoid language conflicts.

(3) The Academic Layer

The formulating of the language planning in the field of law is highly professional which requires a wide participation of the specialists and scholars to provide firm academic support. The academic layer includes academic group, the scientific research institution in the universities, scholars and students.

With respect to academic groups, there are many scholars majoring in the law language associated with the linguistics and the law from the China Association of

Forensic Linguistics subordinated to the Rhetoric Society of China and the China Association of Forensic Linguistics subordinated to the China Behavior Law Association who have yield many achievements on the language corpus planning, acquisition planning and the spreading planning in the field of law but on the opposite when comes to status planning research especially on the language conflicts, language rights and interests.

With respect to scientific research institution in the universities, at present, China has built two language policy research centers in succession. One is the China center for Linguistic and Strategic Studies in Nanjing University, the other is the Research Center for Foreign Language Strategy in Shanghai International Studies University. The main research object of the former one is the language policies of Mandarin and languages of Chinese minority ethnic groups, and the latter is the foreign language policies. The language life research in the field of law requires the integrated knowledge of linguistics and law as well as the cooperation of linguistic and law specialists. The compound knowledge structure and the compound research group are the basic conditions to do scientific research of the language life in the field of law. Therefore, the scientific research organizations of the universities whose leading disciplines are linguistics or law should be encouraged to build language planning research centers or collaborative innovation center in the field of law.

With respect to scholars, at present, the language life research in the field of law is mainly carried out by the linguistic specialists and the research objects are mainly on linguistic and grammatology. This "single paradigm" hindered the further research and the application of the research achievements in the practical field. Generally, the language life researchers in the field of law abroad have received double education, the related discipline of linguistics and law. Therefore, the compound language life researchers in the field of law play a key role in this layer which could function as a catalyzer when the language policy is put into practice in the related areas.

With respect to students, doctors, graduate students, and part of the undergraduates with outstanding creativity are the main body as well as the main subject and executor of the language planning, and the leading force in the future in particular. The complexity and compound feature of the language planning in the field of law result to the urgent need of cultivating outstanding compound research talents with international vision and a good command of language and law. This is also the new subject facing the language education planning in the field of law.

2. Language Problems in the Field of Law

Spolsky (2004), an Israeli linguist, proposed that the study of language planning and language policies has the nature of trinity, for instance, including language practice, language beliefs and language management. The study of these three aspects covers major problem areas in the field of law in China while each area can be further divided into a number of subareas.

(1) Language Practice

The concrete language practice in the field of law in China is mainly language legislation that includes four language behavior problems, which are language use, language choice, language rights and language specification. For example, there are many new problems that worth our research and study, such as the language situation in the field of justice, the language rights of minorities and the protection of cultural diversity within the linguistic ecosystem, the standardization of legislative language and legal translation and so on.

(2) Language Beliefs

It mainly includes the language beliefs or language ideology of individuals and groups in the field of law, involving judges, attorneys and other profession jobholders' language attitudes, language identity, language values, language security and other important problems related to language sociopsychology. For example, problems are like language attitudes and identity adaptation of judges and attorneys when handling cases concerning foreign interests, cases involving minorities or in a court trial in ethnic minority regions, and correct language values, the maintenance of language security as well as language identify.

(3) Language Management

Language management. It is to make an explicit language plan or policy for the problem of language use and spreading, and make statements, which are usually formal documents, but not always. Language management can apply to individual language units, a group of language units, and also one specific or concrete language variety (Spolsky 2011). Subjects with different levels will standardize and manage language behavior of themselves or groups by language management in the process of language planning in the field of law. Therefore, what embodies explicit language policies are laws, regulations, rules and professional standards, etc. And what embodies implicit language policies are the actual context, discourse value and so forth. Effectiveness evaluation and correction mechanism are major problem areas in the actual process of making language management.

3. Legal Language Planning in China

Based on the research and analysis of language problems in diversified subjective levels and problem areas, measures and suggestions are proposed, which all about the improvement of language competence in the field of law in China, and channels, approaches and the mechanism of problem solving.

Firstly, language status planning in the field of law is an important part in the identity construction of China, a unified multi-ethnic country. When determining the legal status of Mandarin and standardized Chinese characters, the study of language rights and ecology of minorities should also be enhanced; planners should attach importance to minorities' right to use their native languages in court proceedings, which is not only a matter of public credibility of the judiciary but also the country image and human rights protection.

Secondly, language corpus planning in the field of law is mainly to study legal terms planning, standardization of legal language, scientization of legislative procedure, standardization of legal translation, modernization and informationization planning and other issues. And compound research teams involving multi-disciplines should be formed while modern research methods should be used. In this way, research results can effectively apply to law, education and other fields.

Thirdly, the acquisition planning of legal language includes policies of curriculum and teaching, planning of teacher training, teaching materials, resources and language services, and other practical problems; as different regions and fields have different needs of legal language professionals, a scientific and dynamic research system of legal language teaching planning should be established.

Lastly, the essential task of legal language spreading planning is to add the value of Chinese legal language. Sapir (1921) regards language as a kind of culture. So increasing its communicative, economic, and diplomatic values is an important part in the soft power building of Chinese culture, and also a basic guarantee of the effective spreading of Chinese legal language.

9.4 Conclusion

Linguists have played relatively closer attention to the study of corpus and language teaching for a long time. However, the research on language situation in law and other fields is not adequate. Even though a part has been studied, much of the interest was centered on special words and other special language phenomena. Their objective is to correct mistakes and adjust vulgarism without realizing the need to conduct comprehensive observation and in-depth analysis of language situation in a certain field, and the need of a systematic language planning. The author holds the view that the study of language problems in the field of law and policies in China and the solving of language problems related to the field of law can promote the harmony of legal language life, advance the development of interdisciplines of linguistics and jurisprudence (such as forensic linguistics, linguistic jurisprudence, legal translatology and so on), and can also further improve the subject system of linguistics. Therefore, with the review of domestic and international studies in this field, this paper puts forward an analytical framework of language planning based on diversified subjective levels and various areas and hopes to promote the in-depth studies in this field in China.

References

Brierly, J. L. (1942). *The law of nations* (3rd ed.). Humphrey Milford, Oxford University Press.

Cooper, R. (1989). *Language planning and social change*. CUP.

Dong, S. (1997). *English for law*. Fudan University Press.

Dong, X. (2004). Research on the vagueness of English legislative language and its removal. *Foreign Languages and Their Teaching, 2*, 60–63.

Dong, X. (2006). A jurisprudent analysis on fuzziness in Chinese legislative language. *Applied Linguistics, 4*, 82–87. https://doi.org/10.16499/j.cnki.1003-5397.2006.04.012

Dong, X. (2007). A legal sociological research on fuzziness in legislative languages. *Journal of Henan University (Social Science), 4,* 74–79. https://doi.org/10.15991/j.cnki.411028.2007.02.015
Dong, X. (2009). *Comprehensive course for legal English*. Fudan University Press.
Dong, X. (2011a). *Translation for legal texts*. University of International Business and Economics Press.
Dong, X. (2011b). *Course for professional legal English—U.S. law and legal system*. Tsinghua University Press.
Dong, X. (2013). Legal sociology analysis on standardization of the Chinese legislative language. *Gansu Theory Research, 3,* 88–92.
Du, J. (2008). *Reading course of English for law*. University of International Business and Economics Press.
Du, J., Zhang, F., & Yuan, L. (2004). Problems of English translation of China's laws and regulations and their solution. *Chinese Translators Journal, 3,* 74–78.
Edington, W. (1994). Language revitalization planning within a power/solidarity framework. *Current Issues in Language Planning, 2,* 239–246.
Fishman, J. A. (1966). *Language problems of developing nations*. Wiley.
Gumperz, J. (1982). *Language and social identity*. CUP.
Guo, Y. (2011). *Jurisprudence on language rights*. Yunnan University Press.
Haugen, E. (1968). *Language planning in modern Norway' in J. Fishman, readings in the sociology of languages*. Mouton de Gruyter.
Huchtson, Tom, & Waters. (2002). *English for specific purposes*. Shanghai Foreign Language Education Press.
Karetu, T. S. (1997). *Maori language rights in New Zealand*. Mouton de Gruyter.
Knapp, K., Seidlhofer, B., & Widdowson, H. (2009). *Handbook of foreign language communication and learning*. Mouton de Gruyter.
Li, Y. (2013). On field language planning. *Journal of Huazhong Normal University (Humanities and Social Sciences), 4,* 86–92+2.
Liao, M. (2008). On several problems of standardization of the Chinese legal language. *Rhetoric Study, 5,* 30–36. https://doi.org/10.16027/j.cnki.cn31-2043/h.2008.05.017
Liu, H. (2003). *Legal linguistics*. Peking University Press.
Liu, H. (2009). Merit tropism in contemporary language related legislation. *Applied Linguistics, 1,* 97–105. https://doi.org/10.16499/j.cnki.1003-5397.2009.01.013
Mellinkoff, D. (1963). *The language of the law*. Little, Brown and Company.
Ning, Z. (2007). *On legal instruments and legal language*. China University of Political Science and Law Press.
Pan, Q. (2004). *The identification of Chinese legal language (1)*. Publishing House of an Unabridged Chinese Dictionary.
Pan, Q. (2007). The optimization of legal language and the achievement of judicial justice. *Catena at Law,* L77–81.
Qu, W. (2012). Problems of China's legal terminology translation and its reason reflection—A discussion on the standardization of legal terminology. *Chinese Translators Journal, 6,* 68–75.
Ricento, T., & Hornberger, N. (1996). Unpeeling the onion: Language planning and policy and the ELT professional. *TESOL Quarterly, 30,* 401–442.
Sapir, E. (1921). *Language: An introduction to study of speech*. Harhcount, Brance & Company.
Sha, L. (1997). *Legal English*. China University of Political Science and Law Press.
Song, B. (2006). Legal analysis of the language of law of property. *Contemporary Rhetoric, 4,* 64–67.
Song, B., & Chen, Y. (2009). Philosophy of language and the standardization research of legal language. *Tsinghua Law Review, 3,* 150–160.
Spolsky, B. (2004). *Language policy*. CUP.

Wang, J. (2010). The research of legal language in Chinese mainland from the legislative era to the era of amendment to law. *Applied Linguistics, 4,* 2–9. https://doi.org/10.16499/j.cnki.1003-5397.2010.04.022

Weihofen, H. (1979). *Legal writing style.* West Publishing Company.

Weng, J. (2011). Analysis of legislation of language rights in China—From the language events in recent year. *Tribune of Political Science and Law, 2,* 132–139.

Widdowson, H. (2003). *Defining issues in English language teaching.* OUP.

Wright, S. (2012). *Language policy and language planning: From nationalism to globalization* (X. Chen, Trans.). The Commercial Press.

Xiao, J. (2010). The background and language rights and its legalization. *Law and Social Development, 1,* 59–71.

Xiao, J. (2012). Legislative formulation of language rights and its antonym. *Journal of Minzu University of China (Philosophy and Social Sciences Edition), 3,* 25–34.

Yuan, D. (2012). *Financial law* (Bilingual ed.). University of International Business and Economics Press.

Zhang, Y. (2013). Comparison of legislative language in the marriage laws. *Journal of China Women's University, 4,* 32–37.

Zou, Y. (2012). A view of linguistic philosophy on normalization of legislative language. *Journal of CUPL, 1,* 67–74+159.

Zhou, W. (2009). *Science of legislation* (2nd ed.). Law Press.

Zhu, Y. (2007). *Concise Chinese law* (English ed.). Law Press.

The manufacturer's authorised representative in the EU is Springer Nature Customer Service Centre GmbH, Europaplatz 3, 69115 Heidelberg, Germany. If you have any concerns regarding our products, please contact ProductSafety@springernature.com

Printed and bound by CPI Group (UK) Ltd, Croydon, CR0 4YY

26/05/2026

02116604-0011